The Lady Was A Spy

Pauline Cushman and the Civil War

Tom Thomas

To Pastor Jim

To WOW 6 TGI NWOs

Tom

The Lady Was A Spy

Pauline Cushman and the Civil War

Tom Thomas

Black Oyster Publishing Company, Inc.

2016

Copyright © 2016 by Tom Thomas

All rights reserved to the author including the right of reproduction in whole or in part in written, transcribed, or digital form.

Black Oyster Publishing Company, Inc.

Casselberry, Florida

ISBN 9781523662944

152-366-2944

Author's Note

No person living today knew Pauline Cushman. Historical writings, necessarily, provide all of our information about her life. In 1864 Pauline had someone write her early biography. She used it to promote her speeches and performances around the country, making it a fanciful rendition of her life events.

Official documents of the Civil War often contradicted the sequence of events described in her book. To complicate research, Pauline's spy career wasn't chronicled in contemporaneous writings . . . *spy activities remained secret.*

Dialogue, for the most part, has been created by the author to match historical events affecting Pauline's life. The author has created some fictional characters to replace actual participants whose names were not preserved over the years. In those instances, I have endeavored to adhere as closely as possible to likely personages. In some instances, historical documents treat obvious physical relationships in a less than candid way. The author acknowledges making some presumptions from what seem to be obvious inferences.

Pauline's story is interesting in large part because she touched so many significant persons involved in the Civil War. Pauline's movements are often verified by the reliable histories of other participants.

Her story has been told before. The fanciful biography written by F. L. Sarmiento, and the scholarly work by William J. Christen, while scholarly, in this author's opinion, missed the passions that filled her life.

In the beginning, I thought Pauline was an opportunist. By the time I finished this project, I not only liked her, I respected her. In life, Pauline struggled for respect. I hope my efforts show her the respect she deserves.

Dedication

I dedicate this work to my family.

My only significance is measured by their love.

Table of Contents

Foreword		12
My Sister's Letter	Preface	13
Chapter One	The Early Years	15
Chapter Two	Moving East	19
Chapter Three	Learning Her Profession	22
Chapter Four	Spreading Her Wings…Again	24
Chapter Five	Falling for Charlie	29
Chapter Six	Charlie Flies Away	31
Chapter Seven	Pauline's Flight	34
Chapter Eight	Leaving the Old	36
Chapter Nine	Reporting the Bribe	42
Chapter Ten	A New Proposition	46
Chapter Eleven	Setting the Hook	50
Chapter Twelve	Her Biggest Role	53
Chapter Thirteen	Her Arrest	57
Chapter Fourteen	On to Nashville	65
Chapter Fifteen	Spy Training	68
Chapter Sixteen	The Oath	70
Chapter Seventeen	Make No Writings!	72
Chapter Eighteen	Behind the Lines	75
Chapter Nineteen	Tennessee	79
Chapter Twenty	Colonel Starnes	81
Chapter Twenty-One	Chockley Tavern	84
Chapter Twenty-Two	Wounded Soldier	86
Chapter Twenty-Three	Captured & Brought	89
Chapter Twenty-Four	Message for Rosecrans	94
Chapter Twenty-Five	Fate of Copperheads	97

Chapter Twenty-Six	Pauline's Charm	99
Chapter Twenty-Seven	Shelbyville	100
Chapter Twenty-Eight	Bolting with the Plans	102
Chapter Twenty-Nine	John Hunt Morgan	104
Chapter Thirty	Nathan Bedford Forrest	109
Chapter Thirty-One	Pauline's Contribution	111
Chapter Thirty-Two	Bragg's Treachery	113
Chapter Thirty-Three	The Court Martial	118
Chapter Thirty-Four	Titus and Jail	122
Chapter Thirty-Five	Pauline's Stay	124
Chapter Thirty-Six	Bragg & Johnston	128
Chapter Thirty-Seven	Pauline Charms the Doctor	131
Chapter Thirty-Eight	Bragg Visits the Infirmary	133
Chapter Thirty-Nine	Doctor Takes the Lady	135
Chapter Forty	The Tullahoma Campaign	137
Chapter Forty-One	Titus Gets His Wish	138
Chapter Forty-Two	A Spy Once More	140
Chapter Forty-Three	Shelbyville to the Duck River	141
Chapter Forty-Four	Nashville & Future President	145
Chapter Forty-Five	Where Did They Go?	150
Chapter Forty-Six	Off the Field, On the Stage	153
Chapter Forty-Seven	James Ward, & P.T. Barnum	156
Chapter Forty-Eight	President Abraham LIncoln	160
Chapter Forty-Nine	Life after the Limelight	162
Chapter Fifty	Conclusion	166
Chapter Fifty-One	Biographical Sketches	168

Historical Characters
Appearing in this Book

John Broughman - Famous Irish actor on the New York stage in the 1860s.

Laura Keene - Manager of the Laura Keene Theater in New York. She starred in *My American Cousin*, on April 14, 1865, when Booth assassinated Abraham Lincoln.

Charlotte Cushman - Famous actress whose deep contralto voice matched Pauline's. Pauline changed her name from Harriet Wood to Pauline Cushman to capitalize on Charlotte's fame.

Colonel Orlando Moore - Provost Marshall for the Union Army in Louisville, Kentucky. Colonel Moore won a smashing victory at Tebbs Bend against Confederate General John Hunt Morgan. Moore approved of Pauline's Southern toast, opening her spy career.

General Jeremiah Boyle - Military Governor of Kentucky. Pauline roamed the General's waiting room to learn secrets of the enemy.

Colonel William Truesdail - Chief of Army Police. Before the establishment of the FBI, Truesdail led the espionage for the Union. He trained Pauline to be a spy.

General William Rosecrans - Union Commander of the Army of the Cumberland. Pauline gathered information behind enemy lines for Rosecrans's military benefit.

General Braxton Bragg - Confederate Commander of the Army of Tennessee. He tried Pauline for treason and sentenced her to be hanged.

Lieutenant General Nathan Bedford Forrest - Confederate Cavalry leader. Forrest confined Pauline as she made her way to her court martial held by General Bragg.

Brigadier General John Hunt Morgan - Confederate Cavalry leader. Morgan became intimate with Pauline during her captivity under his guard. Morgan led the longest raid in the Civil War bringing his troops from Kentucky to Ohio.

Colonel James Starnes - Confederate cavalry leader who attacked and won the battle of Brentwood.

Lieutenant Colonel Edward Bloodgood - Union commandant of Brentwood, Tennessee. Pauline delivered information to him, he ignored the information and lost 305 soldiers in the fight.

General Joseph Johnston - Confederate head of the Western Division of the Confederate Army. Johnston prevented Bragg's dismissal from his post. He later regretted his decision.

General James A. Garfield - Future President of the United States. Garfield befriended Pauline after her release from the Confederate prison. He recommended an honorary commission of "Major" for her. Lincoln relied on Garfield's observations in granting the honor.

Abraham Lincoln - President of the United States. Acting on the recommendations of Generals Garfield and Granger, Lincoln bestowed the title of honorary "Major" on Pauline.

P.T Barnum - American Showman. Barnum hired Pauline to perform in his *American Museum* for several months.

Pauline Cushman

Foreword

I'm writing my sister, Pauline Cushman's biography in 1895, two years after her death. She lived a hard life and finished it with less fanfare than the exciting years of the Civil War. Some of the events I saw firsthand. Some I have repeated from her letters to me, and finally, some are added by me as I learned them in my studies as a history professor at the University of Michigan over a twenty year period. She dealt with generals, future presidents, and presidents, all without intimidation and always with her inborn grace. Always a loving sister, she held a simple belief in our creator, and I loved her. Her strongly held beliefs and actions affected many of the war's major personalities and her sacrifices and brave acts affected several major battles of 1863.

Henrietta Woods Black

Preface

I include herein the substance of a letter she wrote to me. It describes her frame of mind after her court martial in June of 1863.

Two soldiers approached me. Each took my arm and walked on either side of me. They removed me from the courtroom and escorted me to the military jailhouse on base. The jailer, Titus Wilson, opened the door to the watch room. The building was framed with poles and slab lumber. Inside, they used iron straps and rods to hold prisoners.

"Howdy, Titus. Where do you want your prisoner?" One of the soldiers asked.

"Howdy, Jethro. Put her in the first cell so I can keep an eye on her."

Titus unlocked the door to the cellblock so the soldiers and I could enter. The two soldiers placed me inside the cell, shut the door and invited Titus to turn the key in the lock. Titus took the large key from his back pocket, turned it in the lock and walked out of the cellblock with the two guards.

Darkness.

The sun had already set when I walked into my cell. I heard the jailer moving about in the adjoining room. I was alone.

I fell on my knees and asked. "My God, My God, why have you forsaken me?" The trial and conviction of Jesus, the truly innocent one, flooded my mind. I prayed.

"Lord I so wanted to make a difference. I didn't want one man to own another; I didn't want one man to beat another." I stood in the silence. "Why did I give up my life as an actress? For this? Why did I listen to Colonels Moore and Truesdail . . . to be hung?" I placed my hands on the rusty, musty bars of my cell. "How did I go from a tomboy kid to this?"

Pauline and I shared many letters over our lifetime. The events of her spy life were chronicled in twelve letters sent through the spy drop system to David Ellis, and then to my home in Grand Rapids.

The following is my recollection of how she made her journey.

Chapter One

The Early Years

My father, Henri Woods, lay asleep by his bedroom window, oblivious to the worries of late morning. He slept until the sun shone high and then he sat on our New Orleans porch. The shining sun soon scorched our sliver- filled floor boards. The breeze from nearby Lake Pontchartrain gave the only relief that September day in 1843.

My sister, Harriet, sprinted down the street with six boys scurrying behind her. Dust rose from the dirt path as the chase went on. Harriet sprang to the porch and slammed into her father's chest.

"Pere', those white boys chased me home." Harriet's golden Creole skin glistened. She sweated and shook with great sobs.

"My sweet suga-cane, you gots ta 'member you ain't no nigra' but you ain't one a dem fancy white folks neither."

"I played nice to them Pere', why they mean to me?"

Harriet hugged her daddy's waist and hid her ten-year-old Creole head in his soft shirt.

"Hating folks 'cause their skin's a different color's wrong. Don't matter which color do the hatin'. It's jus' wrong," Our Pere' said as he stroked Harriet's hair."

Harriet crawled to Pere's lap.

"I don't want to leave New Orleans, Pere', do we have to go?"

Our Pere' took me under his one arm and Harriet under the other.

"I lost all my money here, suga-canes; I'm takin' you girls outta' here. We gwain' north. Nobody pick on you girls 'cause your skin ain't pink in Michigan."

In December our Pere' packed up Momma and us and the boys to start a new life in Grand Rapids. Harriet, being two years older, watched over me and protected me when our Pere' started hitting walls and kids. Once Pere' took a swat at me and Harriet stepped in the way of the swat. It landed on her back and she fell into our couch. She wanted to cry. Tears were in her eyes, but they never fell. When Pere' left the room I ran to my sister and hugged her.

"Don't you worry, my sweet Sis, I'll always watch out for you," Harriet said. I cuddled in her arms and felt the warmth of being cared for. The kind of warmth we both missed after she went away. I guess that was when I first realized I loved her. Even after she left, she watched over me. Her letters told me about her life, but so much was about encouraging me to live a life that mattered, to go to college when women didn't go to college. She wanted me to have children and hold them close. When I write to tell you about my Sister's life, I feel that warmth again.

Our Spanish Pere loved with exuberance and fought with intensity.

Harriet, tough on the outside, possessed a sensitive soul. She loved to be loved by her Pere' but shrank away when he beat us children.

Harriet turned to boys when he rejected her and turned to other passions. She dressed like a boy and ran faster than most of them. She could beat up me and two of her brothers, Will and Darrell. Jonas, the oldest, never challenged her when she was mad.

The Ottawa Indian boys became Harriet's favorite playmates in Grand Rapids. We went to our swimming hole at the village's end the first week we lived in our new home.

"Hey, paleface girl, who showed you how to swim?" A dark-haired, dark-eyed boy shouted.

"I can swim faster'n you and run faster too," my brash sister bellowed.

"Let's see about that, golden girl." The Indian boy stood next to her, tall and taut and handsome.

"Come on skinny boy," Harriet said.

The other boys marked a race track with a starting and finishing line.

Harriet asked, "What's your name boy?"

"I'm Abram."

"Well, Abram, you're about to be whupped by a girl," Harriet said.

"On your mark, get set . . ." Before the word "go" came from the caller's lips, Harriet tromped down on Abram's foot and took off down the track. She didn't beat him, but she almost made him look bad.

After that, Harriet learned to shoot a bow and arrow, hunt, swim, dance, and fight better than her brothers and me. She learned to ride a horse with no saddle. We shared a family horse. Over the next few years we all became expert scouts.

Harriet fell for her track star, the sweetest of the Ottawa Indian boys, Abram Abanaw. He was two years older than Harriet. They were always in each other's arms over the next couple of years.

"I love you Abram."

"I love you too, Harriet. If you really love me, you'll give yourself to me . . . completely." So Abram said to Harriet every time they were together. She said to him, "I'll be a woman soon, Abram. You gonna' love me as your woman?" On her seventeenth birthday she became a woman with the help of her worldly Ottawa brave.

"Got that gal good," Abram said to his buddies. Harriet heard him. Abram said it one too many times. Our Pere' heard him.

"I'm gwain beat you silly, Miss suga-cane, you shame your Pere' good," Pere' said. He flailed his hands above his head. Henri grabbed his razor strop from the bathroom door and reached for Harriet's arm. She slipped from Pere's grasp, slid out the door, and used her youthful speed to land on Abram's doorstep before Pere' arrived. Her lover's betrayal crushed Harriet but she had nowhere else to turn.

"Take me away from here," Harriet begged.

"Get on my horse. I'll take you to the Wells Fargo Station."

"Will you come with me Abram?"

"I can't leave my folks . . . I got to support 'em."

"I'm gonna love you forever Abram." Tears welled up in Harriet's eyes. "If I don't get outta town right now, my sweet Pere' gonna brain us both. You get yourself hid." Harriet bowed her head, made the sign of the cross over her face and breast and pulled Abram close to her.

Harriet ran from Abram, her father, mother, brothers and me with a kiss and a hug. Our French Momma never filled a big part of Harriet's life, but when she left, Momma cried. My sister wouldn't see her parents again. She wrote letters to each of us. Nobody wrote to her except me, and I wrote to her secretly. Harriet shamed Pere' so much for losing her virginity to an Indian, no one could write to her. In my first letter, I told Harriet that Abram found another girlfriend on the reservation. Apparently she had been around Abram before Harriet ever left town.

Harriet carried twenty-three dollars and fifty cents in her purse from betting and racing with Indian boys, and a satchel full of clothes she hid in case she needed to run from our crazy Pere'.

Harriet escaped her father but Abram's luck ran out. In the same letter, I told her Pere caught the young Indian. Pere broke some parts of the young man's body and caused him to limp for several days.

Harriet passionately loved her Father and her boyfriend. Neither of them returned her feelings in kind. She said she didn't know if she could trust a man again. Abram's wounds healed but Harriet's didn't. If men used her for their own purposes, she said, she could return the favor.

Chapter Two

Moving East

Harriet rode the stagecoach to Times Square, New York City. She took a fresh outfit from her bag, freshened up in the ladies room of the terminal, spritzed herself with some of Momma's cologne and set out on foot to the nearest theater. She loved performing in school plays and shows, why not try to make a living as an actress? She told me later that she was terrified.

"May I introduce myself?" Harriet said as she strolled into the theater and met Arnold Schmidt, the assistant manager.

"I'm Harriet Woods. I acted some in Grand Rapids and I'm ready to perform in your newest production."

"Good day to you, Miss Woods. What makes you think you're an actress?"

"Why Mr. Schmidt, I'm pretty as a picture and even nicer to touch. If you give me a chance, I think you'll be happy. I can sing and dance and . . . and . . . be nice to you."

She took his right hand and placed it just above her bosom.

Arnold blushed and dropped the papers he held in his left hand.

He stooped to pick one of them up and handed it to Harriet. "Read the lines for the young girl holding the parasol."

Harriet read in her clear deep voice, perfect for stage performances. She swirled, smiled, twirled, and bowed. Her obvious stage presence caught Schmidt's attention.

"I don't know. I'd like to see some references. But . . . you sure do have gumption. I'll give you a chance. Don't disappoint me."

He took a pen from his shirt pocket, a piece of paper from his back pocket, and wrote a note. "Take this to the Whitman boarding house. They'll put you up. This paper will let you pay them when I pay you." Harriet grinned her biggest grin.

"Get on with you, pretty girl," he said. Another man beguiled by Harriet's enticing ways.

Harriet took Arnold's note of introduction to the boarding house used by Laura Keene's cast and crew. The home was walking distance to the theater district and swarmed with young people. They congregated on the tiny lawn. They sat on the front porch and gathered in the double living room of the home. In the foyer of the home, Harriet observed a handsome older gentleman staring at her.

"My beautiful dark-eyed maiden, are you new to New York?" the man said. Harriet turned to him as if there was no one else in the room and beamed her magic smile in his direction.

"I'm starting at Laura Keene's theater this very day."

"I'd like to show you the city, if you'd let me squire you about."

"Where would you take a lady to dinner?" Harriet flipped open a hand fan and waved it in front of her face. She noticed refined women use a fan to lure a man, so she borrowed a fan from the theater. She liked the effect and continued to use it for most of her stay in New York.

"I'll take you to a fine restaurant so everyone can see you."

"What is the finest restaurant in New York?"

"Delmonico's of course."

"Take me to Delmonico's"

"What's your name, lady?"

"What would you like it to be?"

"Well, since you're new to the city and the New York stage, you should have a great stage name. Charlotte Cushman is a grand actress and a friend of mine. Why don't you be her little sister? We'll call you Pauline Cushman."

"That's a delightful name. Thank you. What should I call you?"

"My dear Pauline, I'm John Broughman, the most famous actor in New York."

In fact, Broughman was a famous Irish actor starring on the New York stage. The first night John and Pauline dined together, Pauline saw the glamour of being in John's company.

The maître d' of Delmonico's escorted them to the finest table. The waiters fawned and bowed as they served the most succulent steak Pauline ever tasted. The aroma of fine food filled her senses. The glowing light from gas-lit chandeliers made her smile. Pauline could learn to enjoy this life.

Broughman ran his own Lyceum. He didn't bring her into his own theater, but he made sure Pauline always had parts at Laura Keene's Variety Theater.

Broughman gained fame as an actor, but his real power came as a theater manager. Pleasing him by employing Pauline was smart business. Broughman could return the favor, and often accommodated the folks at Laura Keene.

Broughman was Pauline's senior by twenty years. He was handsome, suave, relatively wealthy . . . and hers. He became her mentor, lover, and protector while she was in New York.

Chapter Three

Learning her Profession

The theater business as people knew it was changing in the 1860s. New York's theater companies traveled during the summer. Laura Keene's company left New York every June and toured Louisville, Nashville, and New Orleans. Pauline loved the audiences in all of the cities but the customs of those cities changed significantly from North to South.

Pauline's dazzling looks made up for any lack of acting skills. Her bronze complexion added to her attraction. She always passed for a pure white lady. Her Creole heritage was forgotten in her Michigan upbringing. Her letters to me, nevertheless, reflected on her youthful pain from those prejudiced kids who chased her home years ago.

One summer day she performed in Nashville. The cast decided to feast on chicken and dumplings at one of the better restaurants in town as a celebration. All of the tables had red and white gingham check tablecloths. Pauline sat at a table near the front door with two young actresses, Amy O'Donnell and Kelly Moore.

A woman slave, stooped with age, swept the sidewalk in front of the eating place's large glass window. A young woman wearing a white silk hoop skirted dress was accompanied by a young man in a Victorian black tailcoat of similar material. They dismounted from a carriage at the restaurant's front door.

"Don't stand in our way, niggra'," the man said. He pushed the sweeper to the ground and entered the restaurant. The black woman sprawled on the ground, her broom bounced to the gutter.

"Excuse me," Pauline said. She jumped from her chair, bolted through the restaurant's front door and lifted the black lady to a standing position.

"Why'd you do that?" The black lady said. "You must be a Yankee."

"I am. You okay?"

"I'm fine now. Thank you, Missy. You may be sorry for your kindness, but thank you." Pauline picked up the lady's broom, handed it to her and returned to her chair in the dining room.

"What kind of trouble are you starting?" Amy, a Southern belle, asked.

"What are you talking about?" Pauline said with some irritation.

"The staff in the restaurant will call you a 'nigger lover.' We'll be lucky to be served."

"You can't shove a woman down without shoving yourself down. You can be served," Pauline said. "I'm no longer hungry."

Pauline slapped her napkin to the table, placed some money next to her plate, and left. *One more reason why one person shouldn't own another person*, she thought, as she left her cast members.

Pauline was a traveling actress, but didn't receive star wages. John Broughman could command $150 to $500 per ten-day engagement, plus meals and clothing allowances. Not Pauline.

She worked regularly. She made more money than most women, even though she was paid less than men playing similar parts. Pauline didn't worship money but she hoped to make enough of it to be respected. She loved acting her parts and the excitement of travel. She always wrote about wanting respect from her fellow actors.

Traditions of the time required women to be delicate, fragile, and dependent. The rigors of the profession, however, required them to be resilient, independent, strong-willed and determined. Pauline was a strong, horseback riding, gun-shooting roughneck, dressed in silk.

Chapter Four

Spreading Her Wings . . . Again

In 1851 and 1852 Pauline's major roles in two plays made her semi-famous in New York. Broughman guided her career for three years.

Apparently Broughman was grateful to have such a tantalizing young woman share his bed. Pauline was grateful to be guaranteed parts in the theaters' plays.

Broughman performed in a new play. The cast celebrated good reviews at a party hosted by investors. Plates of fruits in yellow, red, and orange filled the serving tables. A steamship round cut of roast beef adorned a center table with a chef slicing pieces to hungry guests.

"Will the theater critics come to the party?" Pauline asked.

"They never come to the good review parties because they are never welcome at the bad review parties," Broughman replied.

Delmonico's hosted the party in one of their private dining rooms. A musical trio of piano, bass, and drums played in one corner. The investors watched the festivities from another corner.

Pauline, dressed in a silver colored dress with shimmering rhinestones, stood next to her star boyfriend.

"Excuse me Pauline. Won't you go off with the cast for a few minutes? I need to talk to the big people who pay for these shows." Broughman said this with a smile and a squeeze of Pauline's shoulders. Pauline pulled back as if Broughman slapped her. He didn't intend to hurt Pauline, but Pauline's feelings weren't a real concern of his.

"Excuse me John. If you don't love me, so be it. But you need to respect me. If I don't demand respect from you, I'm not worthy of it. I'll leave you to talk with the 'big people' in your life."

Broughman just stared at Pauline as she walked away. He could be charming, but, he made it clear to everyone around and to Pauline, their relationship was temporary.

She resolved not to be hurt by his attitude again. One night the Laura Keene Theater held a party for the cast and the orchestra musicians. She loved a party and loved musicians in particular. When Laura Keene attached her name to anything, even a cast party, only the best was served.

Champagne flowed and caviar was plentiful. Pauline decided she liked both. The orchestra's banjo player performed a beautiful medley of New Orleans style music. The banjo player was a young man from Cleveland, Ohio, Charlie Dickinson. Charlie was a tall tree trunk of a man. He was handsome, charming, and young.

"Can I give you this glass of champagne, or aren't you allowed to drink when you play?" Pauline's gold sequined dress showed off her fabulous figure.

"I'm not allowed, but my mother isn't here. Will you tell her if I do?"

Pauline tilted her head back and laughed with a deep throated contralto sound that thrilled the man who heard it.

She handed the bubbling drink to Charlie, turned away and said over shoulder, "I promise not to tell your mother anything you do, young banjo player. I'll be happy to give you a refill when you take your break." Charlie took a break from the band but not from Pauline.

Pauline lost her innocence a while ago but this was different. Charlie was her age. She had always been with an older man. Charlie loved to laugh and party. His energy and exuberance matched Pauline's. Abram was older. John was older. They all tolerated Pauline's sense of adventure and her sense of humor. Charlie shared it. Not only was Charlie dreamy and funny, his connections in New Orleans, Pauline's long lost home, would bring Pauline to the city of her dreams.

* * *

"My band is playing at the Academy of Music for a month. Can you sing?"

"If you're playin' pretty boy, I'm singin'."

"Come sing with me, my little chickadee, and we'll wow them together in New Orleans."

Charlie could be a wild man on the road but his family hailed from a strict Lutheran family in Cleveland, Ohio. He traveled to New York a year before Pauline's arrival. Charlie left Cleveland to show his famous musician family, his father and uncle, in particular, he could swim in a bigger pond and be successful. He went swimming with the prettiest girl he ever met. Charlie also swam with a lot of alcohol. He partied with anyone, or by himself. Pauline loved the alcohol and the party. She wanted to bed this man. She let herself care once more.

Charlie obliged.

"I'll travel with you Charlie, if you treat me well."

"Pauline, you are the prettiest bird. I want to fly with you everywhere. If you stay with me, I'll sing to you every day."

Pauline stood on her tip-toes and kissed Charlie on the lips . . . a full deep kiss that mesmerized the young bird-lover.

"I'll pack my bags, say my goodbyes to John and the folks at Laura Keene. Friday morning I'll be at your door." Pauline spent the night with Charlie in Charlie's apartment.

John Broughman would often be gone overnight, Pauline returned the favor. When she entered their flat in the exclusive Brownstone Mansion they called home, John exploded.

"Where have you been? I've been up since two a.m." John circled Pauline inspecting her from front to back.

"Were you hurt, did you have an accident, were you robbed, were you raped? Where have you been?" John's eyes swelled, his face flushed, and the rims of his eyes burned from rubbing.

Pauline hung her overcoat on the mahogany clothes tree hanging in the hall.

"John, I never asked you anything when you came home late, or didn't come home for the night. I certainly didn't think it mattered to you if I did the same."

John sat on the Victorian Rococo rosewood couch with tufted back. He jumped up and raised his chin in an aristocratic pose.

"I won't have this Pauline. What'll people think of me if they see you out at all hours? How do I explain this to my friends?" Pauline struck a similar pose with her chin out and hands on her hips.

"Why is it men who make all the decisions in a relationship are the ones who blame you when things don't work out?" Pauline spit her words out slowly in a low whisper.

Pauline circled John. She put her hands on his chest and placed her face close to his.

"In the three years I've been a faithful woman to you, you've been unfaithful to me, often with starlets, and right in front of my nose. What did they think of me, more importantly, what did you think of me?"

John pulled back and straightened to his full height, his clothes still wrinkled from sleeping in them.

"I'm a man and a star. People expect me to be glamorous and . . ."

"And unfaithful?" Pauline inserted. Pauline put her left hand on his chest.

"I may not have loved you John Broughman but I never brought you shame. You saw I worked and provided a roof over my head. I'm truly thankful for all the clothes, parties, and fine lifestyle you showed me. But I think I repaid you with my conduct and my loyalty."

Pauline took out her traveling trunk, dusty from sitting in the same corner for three years. She opened the leather case and started packing her things. John followed her around the apartment taking things out of her case as fast as she could put them in. Pauline stopped packing and walked over to her lover and mentor.

"We filled our yesterdays with laughter. Let's not make today bad just because we won't have tomorrows. You'll have another young thing to hang on your arm before I'm down the block." Pauline put her arms around John and kissed him on the cheek.

She hugged him the way she would hug her father.

"I found a young man my age crazy about me. You are so handsome, famous, and rich. I'm thankful we shared so much for so long." Pauline stepped back, smoothed John's vest and touched his cheek. John paused. He took her hands in his.

"I didn't think I could keep you as long as I did. You thought I didn't love you, but I did." John rolled up his shirt sleeves, took his handkerchief from his pocket and wiped his eyes once more. "I enjoyed pretending I didn't care too much. I suppose the vain actor in me took over. I'm sorry."

"Love doesn't know its depth until the hour you say goodbye." Pauline quoted a line from a play. John took his suit coat from the chair and put it on.

"I'm going out for breakfast. I don't do goodbyes well. Here's some extra cash for you." John put a large envelope on the dresser and turned to her before shutting the door. Pauline blew him a kiss and watched her famous man fade from her life. She dropped to her knees, bowed her head, and prayed for just a moment. She continued to pack but now she hummed a song in her deep contralto voice.

The words came from a new variety show. She sang,

"Maybe I'm gonna' hurt, and maybe I'm gonna' cry, I'll let go of the things I loved just to get to the other side. And baby, sometimes moving on with life starts with the word, 'Goodbye.' "

Chapter Five

Falling For Charlie

Pauline left her famous actor and the New York stage, and traveled south with Charlie. Charlie meant more to Pauline than her career. More than other men, parties, and stage lights. The first night in New Orleans Pauline took in the smells of the French Quarter. The etouffees, jambalayas, and file gumbo dishes gave off aromas and memories of her childhood. The couple stayed in the new, luxurious, St. Louis Hotel, compliments of John Broughman.

Charlie learned to drink Sazeracs, Antoine Peychaud's concoction of cognac, absinthe, Peychaud's bitters, and sugar. Pauline experienced Antoine's for the first time.

"For my first dish, I'd like *Chair de crabes ravigote,* and then I'd like *Crabes mous frits.*" Pauline liked to read the menu as much as she enjoyed having Creole food again. Charlie played many of instruments well, excelling in harp, clarinet, and banjo. Charlie joined the strolling band that played among Antoine's customers for brunch.

Their joyful months back in Pauline's home city abruptly ended when Pauline learned about her pregnancy.

Charlie said, "We can't raise our child in a city as wild as New Orleans. We need to be among God-fearing people."

"Charlie, these folks are sweet and I feel so much at home. We'll find a way," Pauline said.

"Look, darlin', it's harder and harder to be a Northerner in the South. You can't stand the treatment the colored musicians get, and I find it harder to find work in this town."

Pauline worked more than Charlie. Charlie missed band jobs when he drank too many Sazeracs, but blamed his problems on other things beside alcohol.

"Let's go home to Momma, darlin'. We'll make a new life in Cleveland." They moved to Cleveland and married on February 7, 1853. That year Pauline celebrated her twentieth birthday. Pauline did some acting in local theaters and after the loss of their first child at birth, bore two children, son Charles Jr. in 1858 and daughter Ida in 1859.

Sometimes the family lived on their own, but mostly Pauline and Charlie couldn't afford their own place. Charlie would earn good money giving music lessons and playing in the local dance halls, but Charlie often drank his way back home, losing his money along the way.

Pauline had spent three years in a New York City mansion with the finest clothes, perfumes of lilacs and tulips, foods prepared by five star chefs and nights filled with the aromas of Broadway. Now Pauline and Charlie accepted the charity of Charlie's parents and lived in their home. Pauline loved Charlie. Sweet when sober, but not so sweet on many occasions. Momma loved Charlie and his kids, but not so much Pauline.

"Pauline, that hussy, pregnant before marriage . . . that vagabond, that trollop . . . that, that . . . actress."

Chapter Six

Charlie Flies Away

Patriotism drove the social fiber of Cleveland, Ohio. The city provided thousands of troops to the Union Army, and millions of dollars in supplies, equipment, food, and support to the soldiers.

Patriotism ruled the social fiber of the Dickinson family. Charlie's father, uncle, and brothers volunteered for the war.

In 1862 Charlie enlisted as a musician in the 41st Ohio infantry. "Charlie, do you have to go to war? You're a lover and musician, not a fighter."

Charlie stomped around their bedroom, gathering his clothes and banjo.

"My Poppa's going, my brothers are going, and my Uncle's going. I'm gonna join 'em. We're a family, and our family's goin' to war."

"Charlie, if you have to fight in the war, that's one thing. If you're fighting against slavery, that's another. You're leaving little Charlie, Ida and me to play banjo?" Pauline felt betrayed again.

Abram, the Indian boy would rather brag about his conquest than respect her love. Charlie would rather go and play with his Father and leave her with his mother, who hated her.

Twenty-nine-year-old Charlie loved traveling the country when he played in theaters. Charlie saw this as another traveling adventure.

"Take care of the kids and love me in your heart 'til I'm back in your arms, chickadee." Charlie gave her a squeeze, scooped up the little ones for a hug, and swung his backpack over his shoulder. Charlie hadn't been there for Pauline in many ways during the eight years they lived in Cleveland. This absence would top the list.

Pauline watched at the door as her young husband, fair of face and strong of limb, walked out of her life. She thought *the most painful goodbyes are the ones left unsaid.*

"Mommy, will Daddy come back soon?" Young Charlie asked.

"Yes my sweet, but 'til he does, we'll take care of your baby sister and send Daddy letters every day."

Daddy didn't come home. At least not the Daddy who went to war. The vibrant young soldier who left, returned a terminally sick shell of the young man who left Pauline on that cold day in 1862.

Charlie mustered out of the service because of his dysentery. He received his mustering-out pay in Cincinnati. Three months when he could have been with Pauline, he didn't come home. After drinking up all of his pay, he returned to Cleveland and his mother's home.

When he walked through his Momma's door, Pauline threw her arms around her man. Charlie, reeking of Bourbon, was too weak to hug his wife and slumped in her arms.

"I love you Pauline," he said. "I'm six foot tall and a hundred and thirty pounds. I lost fifty pounds from dysentery in the fields."

Charlie's mother pulled Charlie from Pauline's arms and said, "Don't you worry, honey, your brothers and I will nurse you back to health. Just don't you fret my sweet."

Pauline stood next to Charlie with tears welling up in her eyes. *He's still gone from me* she thought. Charlie's red eyelids and translucent skin showed how the months of dehydration sucked the health from his body.

"I lost our money on the way home. We'll have to stay with Momma for a while," Charlie said as he propped himself up on the couch.

Same old story. Pauline lived with Charlie's Momma, either because Charlie drank their money away or because Charlie was too sick to make any money in the first place.

Pauline tried to take care of Charlie, but in his Momma's home it was his Momma who decided on the care.

Pauline went to her room and knelt by the bedside. "Dear Jesus, give me the strength to care for Charlie." She raised herself up, and went to Charlie's side, but his mother never relinquished the seat next to her son. Momma cared for Charlie, Charlie, Jr. and little Ida. Pauline might as well be in another home.

Pauline's letters to me grew darker and desperate.

I keep giving myself to the men I love, and they keep finding me unworthy of their concern.

Pauline had a strong young character but she folded against a mother-in-law who hated her and stood between her and her loved ones. Charlie, the man who swept her off her feet, now found himself off his feet. He couldn't take care of her nor protect her from his own mother.

Chapter Seven

Pauline's Flight

The sky wept drizzling rain for two days. Horse-drawn carriages left ruts in muddy rings in front of the Cleveland home.

Inside the house, Pauline stood over her husband, smoothing her taffeta dress.

"Darlin', we don't have the money for me to care for you and the kids. You need to be fed and washed and dressed every day. Your Momma has your brothers and sisters to help you, and money to feed and clothe our two little ones." Pauline wrung her hands together.

"I can't stay Charlie. Your Momma won't let me take care of you, and we can't pay to feed our kids." Pauline sat down on the sofa next to Charlie and put her hand on his shoulder.

"I'm an actress. I can make good money on the road. I've got to make some money so we can support ourselves. I love you, but what if you don't get better? I've got to take care of them."

Charlie gazed with no focus. His body odor reflected his constant trips to the bathroom, and some trips that never made it there. His chin touched his shirt, then silence. Charlie never responded. He slipped into a deep sleep.

Pauline didn't have time to put her plans into action. Charlie died December 8, 1862. Pauline acted in a play the night he died. His Momma held him in her arms at the end. Charlie lived the last months of his life only from his bed. Momma felt the tragedy of her young son's passing and heaped those tragic feelings on her daughter-in-law.

Pauline spent Christmas with her children in the Dickinson home. The family mourned Charlie's loss. If Pauline felt Momma's cruelty before Charlie passed, it doubled down after her Charlie died.

Momma said, "Why don't you go and be an actress? You don't know how to take care of your kids, and you're no good around here."

Maybe Pauline should have gotten mad, or yelled or fought back in some fashion. In later years she would have. She didn't.

Momma gave Pauline twenty dollars. Pauline carried more when she started out from her father's home at seventeen. The day after Christmas Pauline packed up her things, hugged her children and took the stagecoach away from Cleveland. That was the last Christmas Pauline would spend in the company of little Charlie and Ida.

Chapter Eight

Leaving the Old, Finding the New

Pauline was twenty-nine years old, a widow with two kids she couldn't support. She carried enough money to get a ride to the Ohio River. Not enough money to get to Louisville. She had an ace in the hole . . . men liked to be with Pauline. Like the stagecoach driver who helped Harriet get to New York for a fee paid in flesh somewhere along the route in Pennsylvania. Now she found a gambler working the riverboats. He liked her well enough to book double passage for her and him until they landed in the hotbed of activity for gamblers and actresses, the mostly Union city of Louisville, Kentucky.

It was February of 1863. After two years of war, Louisville residents were on edge. Kentucky didn't secede like other Southern slave-holding states. Confederate sympathizers thought if the Rebels invaded Kentucky, most of the residents would support the invasion. If Kentucky joined the Confederacy, the South might win the war.

Pauline read Louisville newspapers, the pro-slavery Morning Currier, and the anti-slavery Louisville Union.

She read that *The Seven Sisters*, the year's most popular Broadway show would be performed in Louisville. She went to the theater where the management hired her to perform the part of Puella, one of the principal roles in the play.

I told Pauline I was concerned about where she would live, but actors found each other and lived in boarding houses with other traveling workers.

Pauline took a room in the Gilbert House, a home owned by Southern sympathizers. They welcomed the semi-famous actress as a long term tenant.

By the third night, she befriended Beverly Sturgeon, a young actress performing in the same play. They became fast friends over the next six months.

One night they sat on the front porch to cool off. The setting sun dropped orange and purple colors from the sky to the dusty roads. The women watched the shards of light as they danced on the half opened windows all along Magnolia Street. The two women waved their face fans to create a breeze. They watched the purple and orange colors floating across the evening sky before lighting the porch's gas lights.

"I'm not great company this evening, Beverly. This is my anniversary date. Losing my husband was bad enough but I feel the sting of my kids, lost to me for so long. I've got to get my kids back. The only work I know is this acting on the stage and charming men. I love acting. I charm men to survive."

"Who's taking care of your kids?" Beverly said.

"My in-laws, who hate me. As much as I don't like them, they'll raise the kids' right. When this war's finished, I'll take 'em to New Orleans where I started."

Beverly said, "I think you're very brave to be way down here where Morgan and his raiders come shooting everybody. You could be up there having ice cream socials instead of raids."

Pauline responded, "This war's dangerous; the kids need to stay where it's safe from guns and roving horsemen."

Beverly said, "All of Kentucky is dangerous. The Yanks control the cities by day but Johnny Reb stalks the streets at night."

Pauline waved her hand-held fan. Beverly wore only a chemise in the early evening heat.

Pauline's fame gave the play real prestige. Beverly told her friends that besides being famous, Pauline's sweetness and gentleness made her easy to be around.

"Did you save this morning's review of our show?

"Yes, it read *'The Seven Sisters continues to please.'* The last two performances promise to bring the biggest crowds ever. Tickets are selling out," Pauline said.

Pauline waved her fan to keep a breeze on her face.

"Miss Pauline, May I introduce myself? I'm Captain Jonah H. Blincoe." Johnny Reb himself stood on the porch steps. Behind him stood another handsome dandy of Old Dixie, Colonel Willie Ray Spear.

"Well, look at you two sweet things," Pauline drawled as the men shuffled their feet at her steps.

"What can we humble ladies do to please you fine fellows this evening?"

"Please take a walk with us Miss Pauline; we have a proposition for you."

"A proposition, are you sure you're at the right door?"

"Yes, ma'am, no disrespect intended."

Both men wore expensive suits and fine leather boots. The men paid a price for wearing their formal attire in such heat.

"It's out of respect we are approaching you. Our proposition could get us in real trouble if you betrayed us."

"Well let's saunter along Louisville's streets and you can propose away."

Pauline squeezed Beverly's hand, gave her a wink, and stepped off the porch to join her suitors. The trio wandered up Magnolia Street and sat by the trees in the park.

"Miss Pauline, everybody wants to see you before you end the play. You're the biggest celebrity, outside of generals, we've seen for a long spell."

Jonah sweated a bit and wiped his brow with a linen handkerchief he kept in his jacket pocket. Pauline swept her dress up behind her and sat on the cast iron bench at the park's entrance.

"You flatter me, Captain Blincoe. I've played in New York and New Orleans, but I'm not nearly the celebrity you speak of."

"Well, ma'am, we know you are the most glamorous actress we've seen in this town. You've been playin' to packed houses for months."

Jonah sat facing Pauline. Pauline reached to smooth Jonah's lapel.

"I'm pleased with our success, but you didn't come just to compliment me, did you? I thought you had a proposition that drew me away from my rooms on this humid evenin'."

Spear, who waited for his sweating partner to say his piece, chimed in.

"Miss Pauline, we know you're from New Orleans. Because you're a star, you could sway some people if you spoke up about your beliefs."

Blincoe continued, "We want to churn things up in this border state and this border town. It's worth some big money to us to have you help us stir the pot."

"What cause do you think I can help you with, gentlemen? And why me? I'm no political figure."

"Oh, but ma'am," Jonah said. "The theater will be jammed the next couple of nights and everyone in town will be talking about you and the play."

Pauline looked intently into the eyes of Blincoe, the wealthy planter turned soldier.

"We want you to uphold the honor of our state, the honor of our way of life. We want you to uphold the honor of those people who want to secede from the accursed Yankees." Blincoe said.

Pauline rose from the bench, turned with her fan waving air in her face. "I think you want to use my career for *your own* benefit and at a great risk to *my own* safety. The price for such involvement would have to be very high."

Willie Ray smiled.

"We know. We're prepared to give you three hundred dollars in

Federal money. We want you to make a toast from the stage once you have the audience's attention."

Jonah stood and placed his arm on Pauline's.

"We'd like you to toast Jeff Davis and the Confederacy. It would show the Yanks that Kentucky's not Yankee by a long shot, and the townsfolk would have a rallying cry to show their colors."

"You know they'll throw me out on my ear and get the tar kettle ready for featherin'?"

"Ma'am, Kentucky is between three slave states and three free. Our railroads go into Tennessee as well as Ohio; our rivers go into the Deep South and the East Coast. Any change in public opinion in Kentucky affects all the states around us."

Jonah pulled on his vest and tugged his French cuffs.

"If we can provoke our secessionist folks to action, we may turn Kentucky. The Confederacy needs a boost from more than the battlefields. We're not tryin' to get you in trouble; we're tryin' to save our way of life."

Now both of the men engulfed Pauline. One from next to her on the bench, the other hovering over her with his arm on the top of the bench. They were gentle and sincere.

"We'll protect you and you'll have enough money to continue south in style."

"The money will last for a while, but I'm going to need some friends in the South. To some, I'll still be a Yankee under my clothes."

Jonah became emboldened by her consideration.

"Why Miss Pauline, I'll protect you as long as you need, and see you meet just the right people."

Pauline reached for the lapels of her tall tempter. She pulled him close and whispered, "How well will you protect me?"

Jonah placed his arms around Pauline's slender waist, pulled her so breasts and chests were one.

"I'll protect you starting right now. My carriage and driver followed us on our walk. Come home with me."

"Not tonight Jonah, but let's see how well you will take care of me after the toast . . . if I go through with it."

The sun slipped beneath the horizon. The little breeze that ruffled the leaves in the park vanished.

"Tonight, gentlemen let me think on your proposition. I'm not the greatest politician, but I am not wealthy and that's a lot of money. I'll speak to you tomorrow evening. If I accept it will be the day after that."

Pauline entered Blincoe's carriage and returned to the boarding house, where she bid the two conspirators good night.

Chapter Nine

Reporting the Bribe

The next morning Pauline put on her best dress and ate breakfast with Beverly in the dining room of her boarding house.

Millie, the petite teenager who prepared meals and served the guests, was pulling cheese biscuits from the oven.

"Would you like some coffee Miss Cushman?" Millie asked.

"No thanks, Millie. The coffee gets worse as the war goes on. I'll take some raspberry tea. Your biscuits smell great. I'll have one, please."

Everyone changed their eating habits since food became so expensive. The cities were worse than the country because all food traveled in from the farms. Often the troops commandeered the shipment before it came from farm to market.

The value of the Confederate dollar diminished to almost nothing, so Yankee dollars were used if gold wasn't available. Barter became a real part of the wartime economy.

"Nobody thinks about how little food we have for women and children. So much goes to soldiers in the field, not enough is left for us," Beverly said to Pauline. "We're all soldiers of this war. We'll eat our poor rations and terrible coffees and teas. We won't like it, but we'll do our part."

Pauline never discussed her support for the Union or the Confederacy. She had played with an Ottawa Indian, because she loved that red-skinned boy. How could you want to have non-white people owned by anyone? Because of their skin color? White boys chased her in New Orleans for being a Creole. Pauline hated slavery. She didn't talk about being Creole and she didn't talk about slavery;

but she knew in her soul where she stood.

Pauline left the boarding house and summoned a carriage. The driver wore tattered clothes of a greasy gray material. One eye looked at her, the other slid slightly to the left. He appeared to be too interested in his passenger. She took a carriage ride to the theater district and, two blocks before arriving, she got off and paid the driver. Pauline summoned another carriage that took her to Union Headquarters as soon as the first driver departed.

After paying the second driver, Pauline walked up the stone steps of the building, passed two uniformed guards at the front doorway, and strolled up to the desk where Sgt. Major Victor Robeck handled the inquiries of prospective visitors.

"May I help you ma'am?"

"You certainly may, officer. I'd like to speak to the man in charge."

The Sgt. Major looked directly at his papers, without raising his head to acknowledge the person in front of him.

"What's the nature of your business, and why do you need to see him, ma'am?"

"I'm sorry, officer you must be awfully busy. I can see a big handsome man like you might not have time to help a lady who doesn't know her way around here."

He looked up. No man could look at Pauline and not think about her beauty. She made pretty women jealous. Sgt. Major Robeck, smoothed his dark brown curls, stood behind his desk and leaned forward.

"Ma'am?"

"Could you please tell the man in charge I have an urgent message of great importance to the Union and the security of the City of Louisville?"

"Can I tell Colonel Moore your name?"

"I'm Pauline Cushman."

"Miss Cushman? Yes ma'am, a pleasure to meet you ma'am. I'll tell Colonel Moore right away."

Pauline's celebrity duly impressed the Sergeant Major. He excused himself, and entered Colonel Orlando Moore's private office.

* * *

The Sgt. Major exited Colonel Moore's and came up to Pauline and smiled.

"Please follow me Miss Cushman. He opened the door, let Pauline pass through, and shut it once again.

The ceilings vaulted sixteen feet. Gray walls chiseled from stone cast darkness even on sunny days. A lonely desk sat in the middle of a room more suited for a gymnasium than a private office. A wooden straight-backed chair sat behind the desk. Another chair sat in front of the desk. Papers were neatly placed in front of the sitting man. Pauline entered; the man rose from his chair and extended his hand.

"Miss Cushman, I'm Colonel Moore. Won't you be seated and tell me your concerns?" Orlando Hurley Moore, a portrait artist and violinist before the war, was born in 1827, only six years older than Pauline. He, like Pauline, had lived several years in Michigan.

"Colonel Moore, I'm an actress with the Woods Theater. We are performing *The Seven Sisters* every evening."

"I know, Miss Cushman. You are a popular lady and the town is buzzing about you."

"That may be so, Colonel, but I have been approached by two Rebels who would like to cause trouble. I need your advice."

The Colonel got up from his chair, moved the chair from the back of the desk to the side of the desk. He sat next to Pauline and gave her his full attention.

"Tell me."

"Two men approached me last night. Mr. Jonah Blincoe, and Mr. William Spear, both lately of the Confederate Army. They are retired from the service but they are still active on behalf of their cause." "I know of them. We've been watching their actions for the last few months. Go on." Pauline liked the limelight. She also liked to tell a good story. She warmed to her mission.

"Mr. Blincoe, who is apparently quite wealthy, wants me to use my position on the stage to further his cause."

"Are you a woman of Southern sympathies, Miss Cushman?"

"I am not, Sir. I'm a lady who hates slavery and all it implies. Because I was born in New Orleans, they assumed my beliefs matched theirs."

"What did Mr. Blincoe want of you?"

The office windows were high and built into the stone walls. They were open to let the breeze come through. Pauline looked at the windows for a moment as if there might be some way their conversation might be overheard.

"He and Mr. Spear want me to propose a toast to Jefferson Davis and the Confederacy during my performance. They offered me three hundred dollars for my trouble." Pauline paused to let the proposition sink in. "Of course, I won't do it, because I'm loyal to the Union, but I wanted you to know about the offer so you didn't hear of it and suspect me of being, as they say, Secesh."

Colonel Moore paused. Although tall and lean, with strawberry blonde hair, much of his pretty hair had already disappeared. His fingers were long and almost delicate. His taut muscular body belied his fingers.

"It's my job to know who is moving about the city, and to the extent I can, receive information, know who is a patriot and who is not. I don't suspect your motives or your loyalty."

Pauline received information in this session instead of supplying it.

"I thought you might know me because the play is popular. I am surprised how much you know about me . . . and the two conspirators."

"Pauline, you can turn the men down. You'll go on with your career. You're successful now, and I am sure you'll continue to thrill audiences. The money would be tempting to many people, and I am sure so much money at one time has to get your attention."

"I make fifty-five dollars a month. They offered me almost six months' worth of salary. Of course it's exciting to think about so much money, but I'm here to tell you about the bribe, not accept it."

Chapter Ten

A New Proposition

Colonel Moore had a soft heart for the plight of the slaves in America. He smiled at Pauline as if he enjoyed the story of her temptation and resolution.

"I have a suggestion for you, but it will take at least as much thought as the problem you are wrestling with right now."

"Yes?" Pauline said in surprise.

"If you accept the money and make the toast on stage, you'll have some serious money for your needs. You also will be kicked out of Northern theaters and have your career seriously damaged," the Colonel continued.

"If you accept the offer, you'll be hated by Union people and loved by Southern people. You'd become an overnight heroine to the South. You wouldn't be comfortable in Louisville or any Northern cities, but you'd be the Belle of Dixie. Your fame would open up many doors otherwise be closed to you, or any Northerner."

Moore caught Pauline off her guard. Her dazzling black eyes focused on the paper weight sitting on the desk and then shifted focus to the open window behind the desk.

"Why would I want to be loved by my enemies and hated by my friends?"

"Pauline, how much I knew about you, Blincoe, and Spear surprised you. I knew about you because I have dozens of patriots, men and women who love their country more than their reputation. Patriots who risk their lives finding out information. Patriots who risk being hung as spies and their rewards are only known to themselves, not even their families."

Colonel Moore's words were hitting home.

"You mean, I could make the toast, be fired from my job, and become a spy?" Pauline shifted herself in the chair and blinked several times trying to contemplate this outrageous thought.

"Colonel, I confess this excites me. I've always dreamed about the ladies who dressed in men's uniforms to fight with their brothers on the battlefield. This is exciting, but it scares the blazes out of me."

Colonel Moore stood and walked in front of the seated Pauline. He leaned his backside against the desk. His boots touched Pauline's shoes.

"Pauline, let me tell you what I know. I know you were a kid in New Orleans and a tomboy in Michigan. You can shoot, ride a horse and handle a knife if you need to. Your acting skills have had you play male parts and you're good at it. You wrote a letter to your sister saying, 'I'd rather be thought of as smart, capable, strong, and compassionate than beautiful. Those things all persist long after beauty fades.' You understand real values. You'd be a perfect spy."

There was a "wooshing" sound. Pauline realized it came from her as she took in a sharp breath.

"Colonel, I've played so many parts in my life, I thought I could handle anything thrown at me. I'm not saying "no", I just need to get my thoughts around this. Can you give me a few minutes?"

Colonel Moore touched Pauline on the shoulder. He stood erect and said. "I'm going out to get some water, I'll bring some back for you. I'll take some time before I return."

Pauline appreciated the break. She, the cool customer, found her skin glistening, her pulse quickening, and her fingers itching. How did she find herself in this predicament? Yesterday she read the papers to see exciting lives of brave women joining the war. Now she might be one of them. Pauline opened her cloth purse. Her bag displayed a lovely flower design on the outside and contained her trusty rosary on the inside. Pauline took out the rosary, bowed her head, and moved a few beads as she said silent words. Not for long. Just long enough to settle her pulse and calm her breathing.

"I'm ready for you, Colonel," Pauline said to no one in the room.

Colonel Moore let twenty minutes go by before he re-entered his office. He had a gentle demeanor, kind eyes and an easy smile. Pauline liked his looks. She liked this man.

"Tell me your thoughts, Pauline." Moore handed Pauline a glass of water. She took a sip and held the glass on her lap. The water had a salty taste but still quenched her dry mouth and lips.

"I'm a patriot, I hate slavery, and I hate what we are doing to each other in this war. The war needs to be over, and I need to make a difference. I've been play acting my whole life. Now I can do something real. I'm not going to pass up this chance."

"You know I haven't taken this time with you without my own reasons. I think you can do a great job for me and your country. But let me tell you, this is no game. It's serious and dangerous. As much as I want you as my agent, you need to know you could be hung for your efforts. Soldiers are prisoners of war and imprisoned. Spies are shot or hung. No joke–shot or hung."

Pauline regained her composure. Her smile and confidence, missing over the last hour, returned to her.

"Now you're trying to scare me away? Once I make up my mind, I'm all in. Acting, horseback riding, or spying, I'm all in. I worked hard to learn about those other things. I know nothing about being a spy."

"I want you and I'll teach you to be the best spy in the South. If you ever want to stop, you tell me. I'll pull you out of the field. First of all, this isn't a long time business. You can make a great contribution to our intelligence, but few people can do it over the long haul." He paused a moment for effect, then said, "We think we miss detection, but even good actors, like you, get spotted if they stay at the spy business too long."

Oil lamps needed to be lit in the late afternoon as the sun shown on the other side of the building. An orderly entered the room to light the lamps causing a pause in their conversation. After his departure, Colonel Moore started speaking again.

"Let's get you to the toast, out of the theater, and safe in a secure place before anything happens. My men will guarantee your safety. They'll be at the theater tomorrow night. You'll be escorted away and put in a different boarding house than where you're staying now. You'll see the Southern folks who'll love you, but I'll have a detail of men protecting you in the new building."

Pauline stood. She needed time to work her way back to the boarding house without detection. She couldn't be late for her night's performance.

＊＊＊

Pauline played her part as usual that evening. The director added new scenes to make the last performances spectacular. Yesterday he added "Uncle Sam's Magic Lantern," as an opening scene. It featured women playing thirty-four states, all members of the Union before secession. Pauline played the part of South Carolina, the first state to secede from the Union, the perfect state to make a Southern toast.

Chapter Eleven

Setting the Hook

You had to understand the chaos in Kentucky to appreciate what a Southern toast would mean in a so-called Northern theater. Every day Louisville's residents were afraid there'd be guns fired into their homes.

I wrote to Pauline about the dangers she was facing.

In the 1860 elections Kentucky voters gave Kentuckian Abraham Lincoln less than one percent of the vote. Kentuckians didn't like Lincoln, because he wanted to wipe out slavery. State residents owned 225,000 slaves, and 20,000 slaves lived in and around Louisville. The voters wanted both to keep slavery and to stay in the Union. In August of 1861, Kentucky held elections and the Unionists won majorities in both houses, but Louisville's residents weren't happy with the vote.

Pauline's political views were faint when she came into Louisville. When she was a teenager, she wore her brothers' clothes when she hunted or fished in the woods of Grand Rapids. Her only military thought involved this fantasy of dressing in a soldier's uniform.

"I'll be home this afternoon, Millie," Pauline said as she left the boarding house. "I'm having lunch at Morriarity's."

In the North, neighbors trusted neighbors. In Louisville, the economy was built on the slave trade and many neighbors were pro-slavery. Neighbors distrusted neighbors. Friends lost their friendship over their views on the war. This environment encouraged men like Blincoe and

Spear. They wanted to have Pauline stir up the city. They were about to get their wish.

* * *

Pauline looked at her watch. Eleven-thirty a.m. Pauline waited for her suitors to meet her for lunch at Morriarity's, a popular restaurant near Pauline's boarding house. Pauline sat at a table on the balcony, giving her a view of the street and the people below.

"Good day, Miss Pauline."

"Good day, Captain Blincoe, is your colleague joining us?"

"Yes. He's bringing the money in an envelope. He'll join us in a moment."

"I ordered a mint julep in honor of our day. A Southern drink for a Southern toast."

Captain Blincoe sat across from Pauline. He gave his widest smile when he heard Pauline's words. He hoped, but had doubts that she'd accept his offer until this moment.

"I'm going to order Coquilles St. Jacques, the most expensive thing on the menu and let you pay for it. I'm doing this to help the Confederacy, but I know my acting career is over today. Would you join me?"

Blincoe nodded and kept his smile.

"Pauline, your bravery will be revered by your friends. You'll have thousands of new friends all across Dixie. This isn't a sad day, but a grand one." Pauline smiled back. Her brilliant black eyes and bright white smile lighted up the golden skin that captivated so many men.

Spear shuffled up the restaurant stairs to the second floor balcony. The sun light from the second floor balcony bounced into his eyes, blinding him for a moment. He smiled when he saw the gay mood at the table.

"Good day, Miss Pauline."

"Good day to you, Willie Ray. You wouldn't have an envelope with my name on it, would you?"

"I do. You think this is a big risk but you'll be famous around the country, even more so than you are today. You'll be loved by hundreds of families' tomorrow morning." Pauline raised her mint julep to Willy Ray.

"Life's a risk. The only risk I want to avoid is the risk of doing nothing. Let's toast to our venture."

Willie Ray placed the envelope next to Pauline. Pauline opened her cloth bag and slid the envelope inside.

She thought, three hundred dollars, or thirty pieces of silver. These men have the same motive making this payment; just inflation has hit the amount.

Chapter Twelve

Her Biggest Role

The humidity in Woods Theater clung to curtains and seats.

Saturday night. Union loyalists and Rebel sympathizers sat side by side, tolerating each other. A pungent odor from the gas lights mixed with the aroma of bodies sitting too close to each other. Everyone twittered in anticipation of The *Seven Sisters* last production.

Pauline stood still behind the stage curtains. She thought about Shakespeare's words: *All the world's a stage, and all the men and women merely players: they have their exits and their entrances; and one man in his time plays many parts.* She shifted from foot to foot in a slow swaying motion.

This is my play and my part. God help me do what's right.

Pauline bowed her head for a moment and crossed herself.

She pulled herself to her most erect posture and stepped in front of the curtains, center stage.

* * *

The gas lights dimmed at eight o'clock.

A beautiful woman in a white silk dress with the words "South Carolina" draped across her gown stepped forward.

"Ladies and Gentlemen . . . your attention please."

The theater became silent. Pauline carried a champagne flute. "A toast!" she cheered.

The orchestra leader looked at his musical changes for the night.

"Director, I don't see this on the score."

"It's not part of the changed script. Let's see where she's taking us."

A dramatic pause and then:

"Here's to Jefferson Davis and the Southern Confederacy," she spoke, loudly and deliberately, with all of the stage presence in her command. "May the South always maintain her honor and her rights!"

Pauline, lifted the glass, placed it to her lips and sipped the champagne. The stunned audience sat silent for a minute before reacting.

Even though Colonel Moore had arranged for Pauline to make the toast, he did so at the risk of an immediate uprising by Unionists or an immediate riot on the part of the Rebels.

Moore stationed twenty-five soldiers by the back door of the theater and deployed twenty-five more along the front of the theater, sitting on benches in the park across the street and scattered along the sidewalk on either side of the theater doors.

Blincoe, in the hopes of capitalizing on the expected cheering of the Southern sympathizers, brought armed men in civilian clothes, ready to lead a serious uproar if it could be incited.

The actress ducked behind the still undrawn curtains. Moore had his best soldiers wear civilian clothes and placed ten of those men directly in the wings of the theater.

Once people understood Pauline's words, the Confederates in the audience exploded with cheers. Two men in the front rows took off their shoes and flung them on stage near where Pauline had been standing. A Southern sympathizer grabbed the shoeless man and punched him repeatedly.

"Get that Southern bitch and string her up now." One man shouted.

"Pauline Cushman is the Darling of Dixie," yelled another theater patron from the audience. Everyone stood, shouted, and yelled. Neighbor was shoving his neighbor.

A series of gas lights controlled the theater lighting, brightened and dimmed by a crew of four men. The crew turned the lights up as high as they could go, throwing beams of light along the walls and bright reflections off the exit signs at each door.

The Union audience booed and jeered with the same intensity as the jubilant Southerners.

A near riot. The cast stood on stage watching the bedlam in the audience. Once they realized there wouldn't be a show that evening, the cast shouted and yelled in support of the Yankee jeers. Any actor on the Louisville stage who supported the South wouldn't work in a Union theater again.

"Ladies and Gentlemen, this is a loyal Union theater." John Harvey, the theater manager shouted from the stage.

"Pauline Cushman had no right to say those words from our stage." Harvey had to pull his wits together, he couldn't be thought complicit in Pauline's treason. He lost the nights receipts in returns. Worse if a scandal hung over his theater.

"Pauline Cushman will no longer work for us in any capacity, no matter how famous she is," he shouted. Almost no one could hear him over the roar of the crowd. He broke into a sweat, jumped up and down with a megaphone in his hand.

"Everyone will get their money back. This isn't our fault. We're going to have that traitor arrested."

Moore couldn't have been more pleased at the notoriety Pauline received for her pledge of Southern loyalty. What a send-off speech for a spy career.

Blincoe and Spear couldn't have asked for a better reaction.

An uprising. A controversy. Could it spark the Rebs to retake the city? Would the protest push Confederate-leaning citizens to fight the local Yankee government? In any event, Blincoe thought, a new Southern heroine had been born. Pauline Cushman, star of the great stages of America is now the queen of Rebel women. Beautiful ladies who love their Southern neighbors and Southern life-style will join her as sisters.

She'll be a rallying point for women all over Dixie. They'll stand proud with Pauline. They'll endure this war. That alone was worth the money. That, he thought, and the possibility of something more to come. Now, where was Pauline?

Chapter Thirteen

Her Arrest

Pauline stood by the east door of the stage, right where Moore had instructed her to hide herself after the toast.

"Over here, Miss Pauline," said a giant of a man with a barrel chest and a handlebar mustache. The man wore civilian clothes but he and the three other men who surrounded her were the Union warriors she hoped for.

"Get in the stage coach and stay down between the two men who'll protect you," the giant man said.

Pauline made no sound. She followed orders and moved with her escorts as if the group was one living organism.

The stagecoach parked with the horses facing the back alley of the theater. As soon as Pauline safely hid in the stagecoach, the coach bolted down the alley and away from the downtown area.

Blincoe had arranged for a buckboard and driver to rescue Pauline from the Union sympathizers, but he had no idea the Union would also rescue her that night. Spear sat next to the buckboard driver with only a handgun.

"Captain Blincoe, where is Miss Pauline?"

"I don't know, Spear. I ran up to the stage door and couldn't find her. I told her to wait by the stage door and we'd whisk her away."

The next morning the pro-slavery newspaper headlines read, *Pauline Cushman is the New Sweetheart of the South* and in the pro-Union paper, *Pauline Cushman arrested for sedition.*

Federal troops held Pauline captive. Everyone in town talked about her upcoming fate.

* * *

Pauline stayed at a boarding house next to Union Headquarters.

A Union soldier brought her to Headquarters for "questioning about her Southern sympathies" each morning for the next two weeks.

Moore stationed a Union guard in front of Pauline's boarding house each night.

In fact, she studied espionage each day with the best espionage minds in Louisville. Moore needed to prepare her before sending her off to Nashville and the Captain of the Army, William Truesdail.

Susan Cline, the owner of the boarding house, was the only woman friend she had. One night towards the end of Pauline's stay Mrs. Cline shared tea with Pauline in the downstairs kitchen. White powder sat next to an open can of coffee.

"Why is your coffee container open? Aren't you afraid it will get stale?"

"Oh no, sweetheart of the South, the coffee is just in the preparation stage."

"Is it some magic potion?"

"It's a potion to help the Yankee boys get to heaven."

Mrs. Cline regularly housed the sick soldiers waiting for transport. During that time she laced their special coffee with arsenic.

"I start right out with a small dosage. By the time they've been here a few days, the arsenic in their body saves them the rocky ride home."

Pauline hid her horror and gave a laugh.

"You sure go the extra mile to hurt the enemy. I'm sure there'll be a special place for you when this war is over."

Pauline's predictions came true. Colonel Moore set the trap as soon as Pauline told him of her treachery. Yankee boys didn't come to her anymore. After Pauline departed from the boarding house, long enough not to cast suspicion on Pauline's involvement, the military police arrested Mrs. Cline.

Pauline practiced deception under Colonel Moore's eye.

Pauline dressed as a young man a week after her last stage performance. She walked into a local pool hall near the City Hotel. Soldiers and citizens played pool next to each other. A young man dressed in expensive clothes talked to a man who had a satchel next to his chair. Neither seemed interested in the game of cue and stick.

"Are you fellows interested in a game of nine-ball?"

"Thanks, but no thanks. We're just watching the games and talking about old times."

"I'm kinda doin' the same . . . see if I can take some Yankee money home from these Northern boys."

"Couple of hustlers over in the corner. We've been watching them lose to the country boys on small bets. They're about to raise the stakes and clean those boys' britches for 'em."

"Thanks for the tip. Truth is, I've got some money and I'd like to buy things for my friends."

"What kind of friends are you talkin' 'bout?"

"Jeff Davis and his brothers," Pauline said. "They happen to be friends of ours as well."

"I've got a satchel of money next to me to show my friend, Mr. Smith, here."

"What do you have Mr. Smith that this man and I might be interested in?"

"The nicest Spenser repeating rifles ever stolen from the Union boys . . . if you're interested."

Sunlight broke through the venetian blinds hanging on the windows of the pool hall. The light illuminated Pauline's face. She moved into the shadows.

"I just came into your party. I'm interested in making a purchase, but I don't need to create an adversary of your friend here." Pauline pointed to the man with the satchel.

"I've enough supply to take care of both of you, and if I don't today, I'll fill all your orders within a week." Mr. Smith twitched his eyes so often that focusing on what the short man said presented difficulties. He wore a hand tailored suit of fine material but his features were coarse and his hair greasy. His expensive shoes were scuffed and muddy.

"How much are you asking for these weapons?" Pauline asked.

"I need thirty dollars apiece if you buy ten. Twenty five dollars apiece if you buy a hundred."

"I can take a hundred if you can supply me with shells. We can't get enough copper to make enough bullets for the Spenser's," Pauline said.

"I'll get you all of the ammunition you need for these rifles.

How soon can you bring the money?"

"How soon can you get the rifles?" The other man, no name given, said he had money with him and wanted 100 rifles as soon as Mr. Smith could deliver them.

"I can have 200 rifles at the Pierce bridge tomorrow morning at 8:00 a.m."

"Works for me."

"Works for me too," Pauline said. The three conspirators parted.

Pauline sauntered out of the pool hall, reporting directly to her new boss. Moore's troops picked up the satchel of money, the new rifles and shells, and the two conspirators.

* * *

Colonel Moore comforted Pauline. She took this large step for the sake of her country, but she felt alone in the world. Her old Louisville friends deserted her as a traitor. Her new Southern friends really weren't friends. After Pauline's discovery about Mrs. Cline, Moore moved her to his home. The gentle Colonel became friend Orlando, then became more than friend Orlando. The intimate relationship seemed natural to both of them.

"Will I be able to stay until I travel south?" Pauline asked.

"Yes. I'll keep you and entertain you in these rooms. We'll lie in bed and pretend this war is over. We'll make each other feel so warm and loved we'll chase away the ugliness for a while."

They weren't in love, but they were anxious to have the affection of another kind person. Neither thought they would be with each other tomorrow, but today felt like a very warm place.

Pauline successfully completed two missions. With proven success, Moore let Pauline travel from his arms once again.

* * *

Three days later, Pauline dressed up as a man and walked into the office waiting room of General Jeremiah Boyle in downtown Louisville.

Boyle became Military Governor of Kentucky in May of 1862. He dispatched troops several times to attack neighboring territory and fought the cavalry raids of General John Hunt Morgan.

Everyone needed a pass if they wanted to move around the countryside. Consequently, people with legitimate, non-military reasons for traveling came to this office. So did anyone with illegitimate or military reasons. This office provided Pauline with a treasure trove of valuable conversation.

Mrs. Lisa Ford, wife of a Baptist minister, sat primly in Boyle's office. Pauline, dressed as a male, thought the lady looked out of place and worth investigating.

"Excuse me ma'am, as inappropriate as it might be to speak to you without introduction, I am concerned with your apparent discomfort. May I get you some water?" Pauline asked.

"I'm uncomfortable, but I don't require your assistance, thank you."

"You look like a lady of the South in the middle of these Union toughs, and I felt bad for you."

"My sympathies show?"

"You look like a petunia in an onion patch. Do you need a travel pass?" Around them, a hundred applicants spoke at once. The chatter deafened the large waiting room and blurred conversations between speaker and listener. The noise gave the effect of having a private conversation if one concentrated on the words of the other.

"My husband's a minister. He's waiting for me to join him, but I need a pass from General Boyle in order to travel safely."

"My name is Harold Dodge. I'm a Colonel in the Confederate Army. My job is to facilitate Confederate citizens' move about the country." The lady, guarded because of the man's forward conversation, softened her demeanor.

"My name is Lisa Ford. My husband is behind Southern lines. I have some medicine secreted away that needs to get to our suffering soldiers. My husband is already ministering to their needs."

Pauline loved her male disguise. Colonel Moore provided the outfit. She wore a good quality, but not too good quality suit. A conservative brown striped sack coat with matching pants and vest. Pauline sat in the chair next to Mrs. Ford and continued in a low voice.

"I have quinine and other medicines available to me. If you can secure some funds, I'll get you the medicine."

Mrs. Ford looked from side to side to see that no one listened in on their conversation. She rose and walked with Pauline to a more private spot in the room. Slender and tall, she stood too straight for comfort.

She wore a planter's hat with an ostrich plum for accent. A gingham dress of blue and white completed her outfit.

"Colonel Dodge, you are a godsend. I'm staying at the Central Hotel. I can have funds available this evening." Mrs. Ford opened her purse and took out a calling card. She handed it to Pauline. Mrs. Ford then leaned in to whisper in Pauline's ear.

"Please look at the man standing by the newspaper rack. His name is George Sanders. He's in need of help as well. I met him some time ago in the company of my husband. Please speak to him on my behalf."

Pauline found a smuggler for the Southern cause. The smuggler gave Pauline an even bigger catch. *Just like fishing.* Pauline stood and strolled to the man reading the local newspaper.

"Excuse me Mr. Sanders. Mrs. Ford sent me as her messenger. May I speak to you by the window?"

The two strangers walked to the window.

"I can get you a pass. Mrs. Ford said you had a need."

Mr. Brown wore a business suit similar to Pauline's. He looked about the room to see if their movement brought attention.

Apparently it hadn't.

"I've spent months in Europe arranging for loans from the Government of France to the Government of the Confederate States of America. My contact had a pass for me waiting when I arrived at Louisville. My contact never showed. I'm desperate to get through the lines, as my arrangement is time sensitive."

"If you have documents substantiating what you say, I'm able to help. I'm in our country's service. I won't charge you anything but if you have funds available, the more money I have to buy quinine for Mrs. Ford."

"That's a good deal for all of us. I have $2,000 left from my travels abroad. I can give you $1,000 and still have enough money to get home."

That night, Mrs. Ford paid Pauline money and agreed upon travel arrangements. Mrs. Ford, George Sanders, and Pauline Cushman, in disguise, traveled the steamboat to Cairo, Illinois.

"Mrs. Ford, look at the number of people waiting for us at the dock," Pauline said.

"I loved coming to Cairo before all of this aggression started. I miss coming here to shop and have tea with my friends."

Pauline said, "As a child I loved being on the docks in New Orleans. The smells of the paddle boats and cargo had its own special magic."

"We all miss our special times we shared before the war," George Sanders said. "I've been to Paris. It was rundown for years.

Napoleon made the city beautiful. They tore down old Paris and built new Paris. This could be our fate."

The paddleboat eased its way into a slip coated with creosote at the huge dock. A group of Union Soldiers came on board and walked directly to Mr. Sanders and Mrs. Ford.

"Are you George Sanders?" The young Lieutenant leading the group asked.

"I am. I have a pass from General Boyle." George took the pass from his suit coat pocket and handed it to the soldier.

"I'm afraid I'll need you to come with me."

"And you are Gerald Dodge?" The Lieutenant asked of Pauline dressed in her man's suit.

"What do you want of me?" Pauline asked.

"Please escort this man to our security office." The officer said to three men in his company. They marched Pauline away from the area before they released her.

"What will you do with Mrs. Ford and Mr. Sanders?" Pauline asked.

"We'll take the purchased medical supplies and use them for our own troops. We'll detain Mrs. Ford long enough to dissuade her from being a courier again, then we'll let her go south where she belongs."

"And Sanders?"

"Mr. Sanders is a real danger to us. If he secured financing for the Confederacy, he could extend the war by years. Maybe long enough the doves in this country would quit and let slavery continue in the South. Mr. Sanders will be in a Northern jail under close guard 'til this war is over."

"Thanks. Thanks for your work, and thanks for not revealing my role . . . or my gender." Pauline said.

Pauline returned to Nashville on the next scheduled paddle boat. Another event. Another success for the Union's newest spy.

God I love the part I'm playing, Pauline thought as she cruised down the river to her new home.

Chapter Fourteen

On to Nashville

Colonel Moore contacted the pro-Union newspaper. He gave them a press release announcing that Pauline's seditious behavior caused him to issue an order requiring her to leave the Union within the next two weeks. They released her from "house arrest" and allowed her to find her own quarters. Pauline contacted Captain Blincoe.

"Captain, I'm about to be forced out of Louisville. I will be escorted to the border if I'm not gone in two weeks."

"I'll provide shelter for you in a protected boarding house. I'll arrange for letters of introduction while you stay," Blincoe said.

Pauline stayed in Blincoe's selected boarding house and gardens. While he sent correspondence to his friends in the Confederacy, Pauline studied maps of Nashville and its surroundings.

She dined with the Captain for most meals. They ate suppers in her sitting room; sometimes both supper and breakfast.

"Jonah Blincoe, you are as sweet as a man can be," Pauline said as they sat at breakfast.

Pauline wore a pale yellow silk chemise. She coifed her hair and perfectly applied her makeup.

"Pauline, darlin', your dark eyes and soft skin attract me like a bee to honey. I can't get enough of you."

Pauline said, "If we thought we'd make a stir, we sure made a stir with tornado winds. Every Yankee wants to shoot me. Most of the Southern belles applaud me but are afraid to be seen with me, for fear they'll be kicked out of Louisville like me."

"Pauline, there really is a furor all over the Union and the Confederacy about your Jeff Davis toast, and the near riot you started at the theater. You must be careful."

"Jonah, I knew what my fate would be when I toasted the Confederacy. You need to give me as many letters of introduction as you can think of, so I have some safety when they throw me out."

The Captain lived up to his word. He provided letters of introduction to significant Southern gentlemen as well as information where she might stay so she wouldn't be bothered by roving Confederate troops. She shared this information with Colonel Moore.

The last few days she told the Captain it "was her time" and she needed some rest from him.

Pauline left Jonah Blincoe's house and secluded herself in a home provided by Union Colonel Moore. She bedded Captain Blincoe because he could provide her safe conduct in the South and could give her valuable information about the enemy. She shared her bed with Colonel Moore because of genuine affection.

Two weeks from the newspaper story, the Union Army escorted Pauline to the train depot and placed her on the train to Nashville. Colonel Moore had Union guards escort her to a pre-arranged hotel in Nashville.

Louisville's train depot bustled because the city served as the economic hub for the Union's war effort. Trains traveled from northern supply sites to southern battle sites. Northern and Southern spies crawled around the premises because of the critical information available just by looking at the cargo coming and going through the terminal.

The one hundred foot long main platform for passenger departure boasted sturdy planks and iron supports. The gray sealed wood splintered from the daily traffic of the last few years. The train from Louisville to Nashville always left at 11:05 a.m., the busiest time of the day.

"Miss Cushman, you're being transported to Nashville and from there you'll be delivered to the Confederate lines. You'll no longer be welcome on Union soil," Captain Black said in a loud voice.

"Captain, I'm just an actress with an opinion millions of my countrymen share. You shouldn't be making me a political example," Pauline replied.

Captain Eric Black wasn't a tall man but unusually muscled, his barrel chest and bull neck made him look like he wore too-small clothes. His biceps fit tight within his shirtsleeves and his neck filled out his collar.

"I'm just your guard, ma'am, but I'm authorized to give you an official warning. If you're not out of Union territory by a week from today, you'll be arrested and tried for being an enemy of the United States of America."

"If I'm an enemy because I want peace for the South and peace for the North, I have plenty of company. Jeff Davis said, 'All we want is to be left alone.' I'll stay in the South until my family can live in peace."

Soldiers surrounded her and placed her on the train to Nashville when it arrived at the station. A crowd gathered to witness the send-off.

Chapter Fifteen

Spy Training

Pauline knew the political climate in Nashville. Louisville was Union, even if many Southern sympathizers walked the land. Nashville was a Southern town that had been captured. Tennessee was the last state to join the Confederacy. The capital city's significance as a shipping port on the Cumberland River made it a prime military target. The North attacked the area around Nashville constantly. If Pauline faced danger in Louisville, it was doubly dangerous for her in Nashville.

When the Yankees came, retreating troops destroyed bridges crossing the Cumberland River. Governor Harris issued a call for the legislature to assemble in Memphis, and the executive office moved to that city. In the meantime President Lincoln appointed future President Andrew Johnson Military Governor of Tennessee. Johnson set up offices in Nashville. Confederate soldiers held raids all the time. The head of espionage for the Union set up office in Nashville because intelligence and counter-intelligence passed in the most critical manner within its boundaries.

Colonel Moore had arranged for Pauline to meet with the Chief of Army Police, Colonel William Truesdail. The sons and daughters of the South listened everywhere. A slip up in security could mean exposure and death.

William Truesdail sympathized with women caught posing as men in uniform. He sympathized with women for many reasons. He earned his reputation as a ladies' man. Cushman and Truesdail got along well from the beginning.

Colonel Moore, Pauline's benefactor and mentor in espionage, would no longer be her contact. Pauline's needed additional lessons and skills to keep her effective . . . and away from the hangman's noose.

Chapter Sixteen

The Oath!

Truesdail found himself attracted to the vivacious Pauline, but his protocol, established at the beginning of the war, required Pauline's loyalty be tested. Allen Pinkerton, head of Union Intelligence, developed standard tests.

"Pauline, what did you love about New Orleans?"

"I loved the sun, the food, and playing near the paddleboats on the river."

"What did you love about Grand Rapids?"

"I loved the freedoms. Freedoms from Southern boys picking on me for being Creole, and freedom to choose my own friends, even if they were Indian boys and girls. I loved the woods and the horses, the freedom to ride on the trails and go through the woods whenever I wanted to."

"What do you love about the United States?"

"I love the right to pray if I want to. I love to dance when I want to. I love that I can dress up in boys' clothes, or sing on stage if I want to."

"What do you love about the South?"

"I love the South for its food, its weather, and its slow style. I hate that people think it's all right to treat another person like a pet even if they think they are a gentle owner. Nobody owns God's children, even if that child is black, or red, or brown."

After an afternoon and a following morning full of questions,

Truesdail, confirmed Pauline's loyalty.

"Pauline, you're the kind of American woman who makes our country great. We asked you some obvious questions and we asked you some test questions which weren't so obvious. You've passed with flying colors," Truesdail said after the loyalty tests concluded.

"Pauline, I'm asking you to go behind enemy lines. You'll gather information and get it back to me, as much as you can, as often as you can." Truesdail sat back on his swivel chair.

"God help me, Colonel, I want to go. If you'll give me some more training, I'll be the best agent you ever had."

Truesdail wasn't much taller than Pauline. Over the last several days they'd become familiar, if not intimate. Truesdail stood and put his hands on her shoulders. He pulled his face close to hers.

"I'm ready to take you on if you accept this oath:

'I, Pauline Cushman, will faithfully support, protect and defend the Constitution of the United States and the Union of the States thereunder.'"

Pauline repeated the oath. Truesdail gave his new agent a hug.

Tears ran from her eyes. She had suffered pain and disappointment throughout her life, but all of the tragedies and disappointments she met without spilling a tear. She cried and sighed for a full minute.

"Bill, I don't know if I'm crying from joy or relief, or fear. I know I'm not just play-acting. Not just a spectator to history."

She instinctively gave Truesdail a hug and leaned into him so she could clutch him close for a moment.

This most violent war in the history of the world just found a new participant. Her actions would have consequences . . . consequences for herself personally, and for the millions of Americans who believed in the freedom of Indians, Creoles, and slaves.

Chapter Seventeen

Make No Writings!

Union scouts spent many full days training Pauline. Truesdail gave extra lessons at his home. In fact, the roles might have been reversed during the nighttime sessions . . . Pauline taught Truesdail a thing or two.

"Pauline, I think Colonel Moore made a great choice. You have all the talents to be the best woman spy we've ever known."

"Bill, I'm grateful for the words. I want to be all you think I can be, and more."

"Your greatest asset . . . being daring . . . may be your biggest flaw. You need to be aggressive but not so aggressive you don't live to spy another day."

The two of them sprawled naked on Truesdail's big four poster bed. The mahogany wood had grand filigreed designs. Sheer cotton curtains fell around the bed to give extra protection from flying insects. The finest southern cotton sheets spread over the firm mattress, stiff from being dried in the sun.

"If you simply travel behind the lines and report nothing, all you've done is put yourself in danger. If you find great information but are reckless in getting the information back so you're caught, it's the same as doing nothing. You have to be careful."

"I'm going to bring you so much information you'll beat Johnny Reb and the war will be over . . . maybe next month."

The couple laughed. Pauline's father and Truesdail seemed to be about the same age. Although they became lovers, except for those intimate moments, Truesdail treated Pauline as his daughter. He protected her and wanted her to be successful.

Pauline had long ago given up the idea that having sex with someone carried special significance. She discriminated in her choices of partners, but those choices were for her pleasure or her career. She didn't violate any personal ethics in her mind.

Truesdail was at war and his wife lived hundreds of miles away. He took care of his physical needs with others simply because a warrior made sacrifices and so did a warrior's wife. Protecting his country required sacrifices from everyone.

He described Pauline in his diary: *Pauline was exquisite. Her figure ideal. Her breasts were full, but not excessive. Her waist slim, her hips full but not too large. If a woman could design the figure she would like for life, she would pick Pauline's.*

Pauline snuck a peek in the book while she lay in his bed waiting for him.

He finished his description *she speaks in a voice that purrs deep sounds. Trying to concentrate on her conversation is next to futile.* He finished his description saying, *she is the most desirable woman I've ever seen.*

Pauline put the book back in its place. It pleased her to have someone she cared for feel so good about her.

Training ended the next morning. The couple ended their lovemaking for good. Truesdail took on his fatherly role once more.

"Bring me lots of information, but be safe. Don't write anything down unless you can't get it to me any other way. If you must put something in writing, make sure you hand it off immediately."

Truesdail and Pauline sat in his living room.

"No information is worth losing you . . . I don't want to lose you." Truesdail teared up.

"I'll be aggressive, observant, skillful, and carful. You gave me the tools so I can make a difference." Pauline straightened the lapels of his jacket.

"Being a famous actress can bring success. What you give me lets me be something more . . . a person of value. For that I'm ever grateful."

Pauline flashed her magnificent smile, gave Truesdail a kiss on his cheek, and gathered her belongings.

"One last thing, Pauline. While soldiers wear uniforms and openly oppose their enemies, spies wear civilian clothes to perform their duties. Soldiers are not a threat once they give up fighting, but spies may have information that could damage their captors if they ever escaped." Truesdail gathered his things so they were ready to leave his home.

He said, "Soldiers can be imprisoned. Spies are executed so they can't reveal their secrets."

"Thank you Bill. Are my lessons over?"

"Make sure you never have any written information on you proving you're a spy. You may not remember everything, but you'll live to help us once again." Truesdail hugged her again before they left his home.

Pauline thought avoiding danger gave no better protection in the long run than outright exposure. The fearful are caught as often as the bold.

If my dreams don't scare me, maybe they aren't big enough.

Chapter Eighteen

Behind the Lines

Pauline impersonated a New Orleans-born Southern lady searching for her brother, a missing Confederate soldier named "Asa Cushman." To win sympathy from the men in gray, she'd complain of poor treatment at the hands of federal soldiers, who forced her out of Nashville. The Confederates constantly looked for Union spies, and Truesdail warned her not to ask questions about anything but her imaginary brother. Her task was simply to get behind Confederate lines, find out what she could and report back to him. If she needed to send a written message, it had to be in and out of her hands within minutes. The spy network would pick up a hurried note, but it must be . . . hurried.

"Are you sure this will work?" Cushman asked Captain Nugent, one of her trainers.

Pauline tried not to show her terror at the prospect of traveling through the South alone in search of someone who didn't exist.

"Sure," he replied. "Your good looks and grand style will be noticed by many generals and staff officers. Accept all these invitations but with some hesitancy as to the propriety of such excursions. They'll eat it up." Truesdail and her trainers gathered for the last time.

"Take your first espionage gifts. A spy's tool box," he smiled.

Truesdail presented her with a six shooter, bullets, and small packages of quinine and needles—offerings for the military personnel she'd encounter.

With gifts secreted among her clothing, Pauline left the confines of the city.

**

When Pauline traveled six miles outside the city limits, Truesdail's Lieutenant, Shawn Hammock, met her.

"Miss Pauline, Colonel Truesdail wanted you to have a fast and sturdy animal for your journey."

"What a beauty of an animal. He'll be a joy. Thank you, Lieutenant. I'll call him Banjo, in memory of my Charlie and 'cause he'll make me want to hum a song."

So Banjo and Pauline became horse and rider. Pauline didn't feel so alone, now that she had a horse of her own.

Pauline learned the back roads of Nashville from careful study of area maps. Pauline learned the area quickly. She traveled the path south for an hour. She pulled up to the house of Benjamin Milam, a smuggler loyal to the Confederacy. Pauline's first chance to try out her new role. Pauline saw a woman standing by the front door of the home.

She dismounted and ran to her.

"Are you the owner here?" Pauline stood taller than the lady. Pauline loved her fine white silk blouse and her chocolate colored skirt that touched her shoes.

"I am. I'm Mrs. Milam. May I help you?" The curtain rose on Pauline's new career.

"Oh, if you would. I'm Pauline Cushman. The Yankees threw me across Rebel lines for believing in Jeff Davis and our state's rights."

"I know who you are Miss Cushman. You're the talk of all Dixie. Come in, and let me pour you some tea." Pauline lamented her condition.

"I'm carrying everything I own on my back, they took everything else. My wardrobe, my jewels, everything!"

"I knew they arrested you after you toasted the South. I'm glad to see you released. If they arrested everyone in Nashville who agreed with you, the prisons would be overflowing," Mrs. Milam said.

"I know you're right. I've had a lot of women thank me for rallying our Dixie men in Louisville. Maybe we can take a stand again." Pauline got comfortable in her role. She tied Banjo to a post, asked for some feed, and after feeding and watering the bay, she entered the Milam's house.

The two women sat in Mrs. Milam's dining room. The oval oak table had room for eight matching oak chairs. A tablecloth of crocheted material draped the entire surface.

"Where are you headed Miss Cushman?" Mrs. Milam asked.

"I know my brother Asa is in the Command of General Bragg. I have a letter of introduction from Captain Jonah Blincoe asking the nearest Confederate Officer of a Platoon to direct me to General Bragg's headquarters."

"You're looking for your brother? I'm afraid you're a long ways away from General Bragg. You can't search for him tonight dear. Come and stay with us. It would be an honor to have you under our roof."

"Mrs. Milam, you keep such a lovely home. Did you crochet this table cloth?"

"Yes. I make tablecloths and doilies for my sisters in Nashville as well as for my own home. I don't suppose you have time to make them with your life on stage?" Mrs. Milam said.

"I haven't done so in the last few years. My mother taught me years ago. She died when I was seventeen. I stopped crocheting after that," Pauline said.

"I crochet and bake fruit breads. Benjamin goes into Nashville several times a week and sells them to a store on Azalea Street."

"I walked down Azalea Street often. Perhaps we crossed paths," Pauline said.

"Benjamin is very careful when he's in town. He speaks only to Southern sympathizers. He carries things back and forth for them. He's a brave man and proud of his heritage. He makes a living helping the people who need him. He can't brag about it, except to me and our kind."

"I know how cruel the Federals can be. They swore and cursed me before they kicked me out of town. He must be careful for your sake."

Pauline and Mrs. Milam talked about lots of other things, and never mentioned Benjamin's smuggling business again.

The Milams were cordial hosts. Pauline slept in their guest room looking out on a garden filled with yellow trillium, red and white bleeding hearts and crimson clover.

In the morning, Mrs. Milam had toast and tea, jam and honey on the table, and packed lunch for Pauline to take with her on the road.

"I've brushed down your horse and saddled him for you. Can I help you with your luggage?" Mr. Milam said.

"It's kind of you Mr. Milam. I'm afraid they let me take nothing with me. When I find my brother, he'll replenish my wardrobe and theater clothes," Pauline said.

"Be careful on your way. The Confederate outpost in our county is down the road about six miles. Good luck in you travels." Mr. Milam said. Pauline thanked her hosts, packed her lunch in Banjo's saddle bags and headed on her mission.

Pauline ran into a group of confederate soldiers and told her story. They directed her passed the local Confederate outpost.

"Darling don't you think it's odd she'd be sent packing for good without her clothes and wardrobe?" Mr. Milam said.

Milam shied away from things that seemed unusual to him.

He saddled up a horse and trotted to the Confederate outpost. He not only thought her lack of luggage odd, her lack of an escort strange as well. When he arrived at the outpost, no one had seen Pauline. More strange conduct. He told the Confederate captain of his meeting with Pauline and what seemed to be suspicious conduct to him. No proof of wrong doing, just a feeling.

Chapter Nineteen

Tennessee Residents' State of Mind

Tennessee had 120,000 Tennessee men, mostly from Middle and Western Tennessee, join the Confederate Army. It also had forty thousand of them, mostly from Eastern Tennessee, join the Union Army.

Pauline's mission was to learn what she could in and around Nashville. Her riding experiences around the Nashville countryside made her a good scout. Pauline was detained by a platoon from the Confederate 38th Tennessee Division on the road from Nashville to Memphis.

Pauline said to the young horseman who led the group, "I'm Pauline Cushman. I'm the actress kicked out of Louisville because I toasted the South." Pauline teared up, paused, and then continued, "My brother, Asa, is an officer with General Bragg's troops. Can you help me find him?"

The lead soldier spoke.

"I'll leave you with my men, ma'am. I'll speak to the commander and return in a moment." The young lieutenant touched his glove to his hat and gave a short bow of his head. He spurred his horse, turned in full cantor, and rode to the back of the troops.

The sun shone and danced upon the hills and valleys of the Tennessee countryside. Green trees and wild Iris flowers dotted rolling meadows. The rural splendor belied the blood spilled by young American men at every turn.

The Lieutenant accompanied by a tall, stately looking man,

handsome, Pauline thought, with an athletic face. Bronze skin pulled tightly across his high forehead and patrician nose. Pauline thought the man was a little bit younger than she. A welcome change from all the older men she had to deal with.

"Let me introduce myself, Miss Cushman, I'm Colonel John Carter. We know about you. We're happy to help."

Pauline gave the Colonel her most demure smile and nod of her head.

"I am grateful for your kindness Colonel Carter. I'll fall in by your side."

The good colonel, being a Southern gentleman and lawyer from Memphis, kept Pauline by his side both while they marched and while they slept for the next week.

By the end of the week, Pauline had learned about relative troop strengths in the area, and the plans of the 38th Tennessee Division for the coming month.

When they parted, Pauline received a letter of introduction from Carter to Colonel J.W. Starnes who held command in an outpost just south of the Village of Brentwood.

Pauline rode Banjo north once Carter's troops marched out of sight. She traveled to a rural post office on the Brentwood road.

Daniel Ellis, the patriot from East Tennessee, regularly delivered information from the field to Truesdail's office in Nashville. The post office six miles south of Brentwood served as a spy drop. Ellis retrieved Pauline's notes describing battle plans of the 38th Tennessee Division. Truesdail read those plans and reacted. Truesdail, in turn, delivered the information to General William Rosecrans of the Army of the Cumberland.

Pauline's information confirmed Rosecrans's hopes. He planned the upcoming battle of Tullahoma based, in part, on her information. Because of Pauline's sacrifices, Rosecrans executed false starts around the mountain gaps that fooled Bragg's forces.

Chapter Twenty

Starnes and the Battle of Brentwood

Pauline sought out Colonel James Starnes. She found her way to his headquarters five miles outside of Brentwood, and twelve miles south of Nashville.

Starnes welcomed Pauline as a Southern Patriot and gave her all the courtesies appropriate to the moment. Starnes was a surgeon. He gave up his surgical duties to lead a brigade of cavalry under General Forrest.

"Colonel Starnes, I'm trying to find my brother, Colonel Asa Cushman. He's stationed somewhere within General Bragg's command."

"We've been told to give you any assistance we can. I've asked my officers if they're familiar with your brother and his whereabouts. I'm sorry we have no information to share."

"I appreciate your concerns on my account, Colonel. I've been searching since Yankee scoundrels threw me out of Nashville. If you'd be so kind, I'd appreciate a letter of introduction to General Forrest."

"That may get you one step closer to General Bragg, but General Forrest and General Bragg aren't friends. You may give that some consideration if you are looking for an introduction to General Bragg through General Forrest."

Starnes was a well-groomed soldier. He wore a full beard neatly trimmed even as he roamed the battlefields around Nashville.

"Please join us for lunch, Miss Cushman. My cooks have prepared a big lunch. We'll be on the move tomorrow, so we're eating a lot today." Starnes said.

After Pauline spent time with Starnes and his officers she learned he planned an attack on Brentwood. Union Lt. Col. Edward Bloodgood commanded the Brentwood post on the Nashville & Decatur Railroad line. Bloodgood had four hundred men protecting that station. Pauline rode from the company of her hosts and reached an outpost of Bloodgood's command on March 24th 1863.

A Sgt. Major guarded the entrance to the encampment.

"Dear Sergeant, I have an urgent message for Colonel Bloodgood. Could you inform him I need an audience?"

"I'm sorry ma'am, I can't reach him. Can I help you?"

"I'm afraid not Sergeant, I need to speak to an officer who can speak to Colonel Bloodgood."

"I'll see what I can do."

The soldier locked Pauline out of the fenced area and left his post. He returned in the company of three officers, including Lt. Colonel Bloodgood.

"What information do you need to tell me, madam?"

"You're Colonel Bloodgood?"

"I am. Please state your business."

"I'm working under the authority of William Truesdail, chief espionage officer of the country. I've learned Colonel Starnes is planning a raid on Brentwood tomorrow. He plans to cut your telegraph lines before ripping up the train tracks. His raid is to take place before the sun sets tomorrow."

"Is there anything else?"

"Yes. He plans on attacking your stockade at the same time to cut off any retreat."

"And your name?"

"I'm Pauline Cushman. I have been placed behind the lines by Colonel Orlando Moore and Colonel William Truesdail. I've made this trip, at great personal risk, to save your company."

"You're the lady who toasted the South just two months ago? I recognize your name."

"Yes, I'm that lady. I staged the toast so I could work behind enemy lines."

"I am not sure which lines you consider the enemy's lines Miss Cushman. I'll take your information under advisement."

The Union soldiers clearly didn't believe Pauline. Bloodgood planned on deploying his men on the other side of the encampment the following morning. He saw no reason to change his plans because of a turncoat. He and his officers turned and left Pauline. The Sergeant Major didn't offer her entrance to the compound. Pauline mounted her horse and trotted off to the relative safety closer to Confederate camps.

The next morning Colonel Starnes found unprotected telegraph lines. No guards protected the railroad tracks. Starnes, with fewer horsemen than Bloodgood, destroyed Brentwood's infrastructure. Later in the morning, General Forrest brought his cavalry brigade behind Starnes. After Forrest and Starnes surrounded the outpost and stationed men at the stockade blocking any retreat, Forrest sent a message to Bloodgood with a demand to surrender.

Bloodgood refused. After 305 of Bloodgood's men were slaughtered, he finally waived the white flag.

Pauline brought this valuable information to Bloodgood, but he chose to ignore the information.

Pauline traveled as swiftly as she could away from Brentwood. When she neared Wartrace she stopped at a general store that served sweet tea to its customers. While she rested the telegraph operator who owned the store announced to customers that Forrest had pulled out another victory for the rebel cause.

"Killed them Yanks, almost every single one," the owner bragged.

Pauline turned her face and stepped out of the store. She walked to the back of the building to an open field, scattered with wild flowers.

She fell to her knees, put her hands on her bodice and said a soft prayer. Dear Jesus, why? Pauline's sacrifices; sleeping with strangers, riding behind enemy lines, and taking the risk of being hanged, all in vain . . .

Chapter Twenty-One

Chockley Tavern and the Boy Hero

Pauline traveled into the night and slept on the ground. She reached Wartrace, Tennessee hoping to catch General Bragg's forces. Starnes gave her a letter of introduction to Braxton Bragg, the head of the Army of the Tennessee, and the man whose movements Truesdail wanted most. The second night she stayed at Chockley Tavern, a two story building that had sleeping rooms on the second floor.

"Mrs. Chockley, my name is Pauline Cushman. I have a letter of introduction from Colonel Starns for the eyes of General Bragg. I'd like to stay with you for a few days while I try to find my brother."

"Why Pauline Cushman. What an honor to have you with us. You're welcome to stay and share meals with us. We'll charge you the same rate we charge our friends when they're in need of shelter."

Pauline desired to be in the company of people with such strong Southern sympathies. This might be a great place to gain valuable information.

"May I join you in the kitchen?" Pauline asked. The cooks were busy preparing for the evening meal.

"Come and join us. A patriot like you will like our special preparations," Mrs. Chockley said.

Pauline wore clothes fit for riding, but still glamorous on her celebrated figure. Two young women and a young man tended the kitchen.

Mrs. Chockley introduced everyone.

"Pauline Cushman, famous actress and toast mistress for Jeff Davis, meet Sam Davis, boy hero of the Confederacy."

Sam was born in 1842, nine years after Pauline. The twenty-one year old spy thought Pauline was the most beautiful woman he'd ever seen. Pauline recognized the familiar adoration and immediately brought the young man into her web.

The boy hero and Pauline spent two days together, talking and laughing. They walked the fields, held hands, and ate every meal together. Pauline poured her charm all over that young man. He melted like butter on hot bread. After going to bed and waking up together for two nights Pauline asked at breakfast, "Why are you so popular at such a young age?"

"Because I'm so smart and tricky," Sam said.

He wore a faded red shirt with white polka-dots. His overalls had only one shoulder strap over his left shoulder. Blonde hair fell over his eyes. It hadn't been trimmed in months. Shoes and socks were nowhere in sight.

"How are you so tricky, you sweet boy with no shoes?"

"I fool those Yanks when I pass by the lines. I put messages down chicken necks, stuff notes in butter knife handles and bury bigger notes in flour sacks. I dress like a kid and they don't suspect I'm a spy."

Sam never knew who exposed him as a spy less than eight months after his time with Pauline. Some spiders' bite is more lethal than their web.

Chapter Twenty-Two

The Wounded Union Soldier

Pauline let Davis fall into a deep sleep the last night they spent together. Young Sam drank more than he should have and became doubly tired from his rigorous love making. Pauline not only used her lovemaking skills, she gave him an extra knockout punch . . . knockout drops from her cache. Pauline donned his clothes as soon as her young lover fell asleep. She snuck from the tavern disguised as a young man.

Pauline needed to get this new information, the name of the young spy and three formidable methods the Rebs were using to pass messages, to Daniel Ellis and his Union spy system. She slipped out to the stables behind the tavern and mounted Banjo without putting on his saddle. Pauline and the Ottawa Indian boys rode their horses bare back for years. Pauline traveled almost an hour when a Confederate officer, in the company of two other Rebs, confronted her.

"What are you doing out at this time of night, Mister?"

Pauline rode about forty yards from the trio. She spiked Banjo with her heels, released pressure on the bridle, and headed full tilt down the valley that stretched below her.

The three men chased her. She jumped over a huge rock jutting out from the slope and landed in the creek bed below.

"Damn, that fellow went lickety-split; let's try downstream."

Two of the horsemen were very young, maybe eighteen or so.

The Captain seemed to be in his early twenties. The trio road their horses at full gallop along the stream as it curved down the valley.

"Lookit, Johnny, there's a shallow spot comin' up on us."

"Get at it Billy John, make that horse fly."

The three Rebs splashed across the creek behind where Pauline had passed moments ago. The two young horsemen were fast as the wind. Pauline thought she could outrace the country boys. Just as she got into a smooth rhythm, she saw a sight . . . a Yankee horseman coming right at her, not fast, but right at her.

"Mister, what are you doing?" Pauline yelled and drew her pistol.

"I've been shot by one of you Rebel bastards and I'm about to bleed to death," the Yankee soldier said.

"You're about to have a stroke of good luck and so am I. I'm Pauline Cushman and I'm a Union spy. Do you want to live?" The wounded Union soldier slipped off his horse and lay near a tree.

"I know who you are, Miss Cushman. I thought you were a Reb."

"Well I'm not, but you need to be captured or you'll bleed to death laying out here." Pauline dismounted and slid the man up against the tree.

"I can save you, but you have to help me with a story that'll save us both."

"I'll do whatever it takes. If you're safe, and I'm not, it's okay. I'll be good, no matter."

The soldier held his hand just above his hip as the blood continued to ooze from his body. Bang! Pauline shot a bullet from her pistol skyward.

"When those Rebs come, I'm going to tell 'em I shot you. You tell 'em it's true. If you do, they'll capture you and let me go free. Otherwise we're both done for."

The soldier nodded. The Rebs swarmed over them in a minute.

"Why'd you run from us, boy?" One of the Rebs said as they pulled their horses to a rest.

"Oh my God, you're Confederates. I thought you were damn Yankees and I ran away from you. I came on this Yank and shot him. I never shot a man before, not even a Yank."

"You get yourself to where you're goin' and don't be out at night if you know what's good for you. We'll get this Yank to a doctor and a prison so you don't have to worry about killin' no one . . . get out of here."

Nobody had to tell Pauline twice. She doubled back to her spy drop, wrote a note to Truesdail, and sped back to the Chockley Tavern.

Pauline put Banjo in the stables, slithered into the tavern, and climbed the stairs. She almost reached her room when she heard noises down the hall. Mr. Chockley heard a sound and bolted out of his upstairs room with his rifle in hand. If he spotted her in men's clothes, he'd be wildly suspicious.

Pauline slid into the hall closet and peeked through the partially opened door. The closet held dirty sheets and pillowcases waiting to be washed. The pile of laundry had a musty smell that filled her nostrils in the tight space. Mr. Chockley stared into the closet in search of the intruder. Chockley swung the closet door open and thrust the rifle barrel into the dark.

Pauline had placed a dirty sheet in front of her. Chockley didn't see anyone and shut the door. After he climbed down the stairs, back up the stairs and returned to his room, Pauline tip-toed out of the closet, undressed, and wriggled her way beneath the blanket to hold on to her lover. When Sam Davis woke up, he thought he died and gone to heaven. Thanks to Pauline, that would soon be true.

Chapter Twenty-Three

Captured and Brought to the Johnson's

Pauline returned to Nashville to perform in a play for three nights. She got the part at the New Nashville Theater on the strength of a recommendation from her old boss in Louisville. He wrote, *she's a good looking woman and an accomplished actress . . . even if she's a Reb.* The newspapers reported that Pauline had been granted permission by the Union government in Nashville to stay in the city and perform on stage for three nights only at the request of the theater owner.

***

Her return to the stage masked her real reasons for the trip. One reason was the enemy seemed to be close on her trail. The other was she met with Colonel Truesdail to be brought up to date about the overall military strategy of the region. Her knowledge needed updating because the battle strategies changed. After her performances, she continued her quest to find her brother Asa. She returned behind lines to meet up once more with Colonel James Starnes.

   Her first night back was her best night of information gathering so far. J.W. Starnes had impressed his beautiful escort by bragging about his upcoming attack on Rosecrans's troops. Starnes learned Rosecrans was taking a weekend trip away from his troops. Starnes would attack twenty four hours after Rosecrans departed and would catch the Yankees without their leader.

   "Colonel Starnes, I'm in your debt, but I need to find my brother. All we have is each other."

Starnes quoted an ancient saying, "Ten men wisely led will defeat an army without a head." Starnes would deliver a killing blow and the South would have a new rallying cry. Maybe even give the Yankees a reason to quit their aggression.

The Copperheads were in full swing in the North. They wanted a negotiated settlement to end the war, at all costs. A victory against Rosecrans might be the tipping point. The effort to eradicate slavery in the country, Pauline thought, might be lost.

"Colonel Starnes, I am in your debt, but I need to find my brother. All we have is each other. As much as I love your company Colonel, I have to continue my search. Forgive me if I take leave of you once again."

Pauline started from Wartrace and traveled south for fifteen minutes. She knew of a turn-around trail that would take her back on the path to a Nashville spy pickup designated by Ellis and his runners.

If she were caught headed in the wrong direction, her letter of introduction would mean nothing.

These were Pauline's roads. Her tracking skills had been honed as a teenager in Ottawa territory. She could read the signs of travel from the dust and debris on the road. She knew a large group of cavalry passed by recently. She'd lay back in the small clump of cottonwood trees mixed with oaks until enough time had passed.

The moonlight shone bright enough to make the outline of a plantation house past the tree stand. If she couldn't stay hidden there, she'd make her way to the house and shelter for the night.

Pauline moved Banjo into the grove and settled behind an oak tree.

"Stand and identify yourself," a voice from the woods declared.

Out of the same tree cover were three confederate soldiers acting as rear guard for the troops up ahead.

Yankees were expected in pursuit and these three fellows were to shoot their weapons at the Yanks as often as possible so the sound would be a warning to the cavalry in the front line.

"I'm Pauline Cushman. I'm on my way to find my brother, an officer under General Bragg's command."

"You may be Pauline Cushman but you're going directly away from General Bragg's command. Do you have any paperwork to show me?" the Rebel officer asked.

Pauline pulled out her letter of introduction. It said she and her party should be given every courtesy in her search for her brother. Of course, Pauline had no party since Pauline slipped away from her escorts in order to reach a spy drop.

"Madam, there's no explanation for you being alone in these woods at night except you're hiding your whereabouts without an appropriate pass. We're taking you to the Johnson plantation in the distance and in the morning we'll take you to General Bragg's outpost. You can explain yourself to him personally."

The jig was up. Pauline knew she couldn't explain away her whereabouts. She traveled too many miles north of where she last traveled with her escort party.

"Of course I'll travel with you Lieutenant. You'll see General Bragg will welcome me. I suggest you treat me as a friend of the Confederacy so you'll not be further embarrassed thereafter." Pauline used all of her acting skills to buy what little time she might have before her exposure. Death could be waiting around the corner.

The plantation had smoke curling from its chimneys and candlelight glowing from its windows. Two soldiers escorted Pauline with a soldier on either side of her and the Lieutenant following behind her.

"We'll stay here for the night. In the morning we'll take you to a Confederate outpost and turn you over."

"When the facts are examined I'll resume looking for my brother, an officer in the Confederacy, just like you."

They came upon the plantation and tied their steeds to the rail in front. The lieutenant knocked on the door.

"Excuse me ma'am, I'm Lieutenant Sharpe, we need to place this woman under arrest in your home for the night. We'll need to stay as well. We'll try to be as considerate of your time as possible."

"You're welcome in our home Lieutenant, come in. I'm Mrs. Johnson; my husband is in the parlor."

The two soldiers took saddles from the horses, piled them beside the front porch and brushed down the horses before coming inside. The Plantation stood much longer than its width. The actual size belied its appearance from the trail.

Mr. and Mrs. Jeremiah Johnson, the owners, had a crop of cotton and a barn behind the main building. Thomas Jefferson, a slave of about fifty-five, lay on a pallet next to a fireplace. Mr. Johnson's first cousin, Andrew Johnson, sat as the Tennessee Governor. Johnson prided himself as a loyal Confederate citizen. His wife's family owned human beings as slaves for three generations. They treated Thomas Jefferson as well as any of their other farm animals, but no better.

The Jeffersons asked the Lieutenant to sit and share some locally brewed whiskey. They abandoned Pauline to warm herself by the fire. Pauline leaned over and pretended to stoke the smoldering embers in the fireplace. Sparks flew up when she shoved the poker under a charred log.

"Say mister," Pauline whispered to the slave reclining next to the fireplace. "Mister, how'd you like a Yankee ten dollar bill?" Pauline got his rapt attention.

"Don't get me in trouble Miss; I ain't geared for any more trouble than I already has."

"No trouble, I just want you to go outside, wait a few minutes and yell. Yell the Yankees are headed this way. Nothin' more. Can you do that?"

"Nothin' more?"

"Nothin' more. See me place this bill behind the wood? I'll leave it there for you to pick up when you get back and no one'll see you pick it up."

"'Nuf said." Thomas got up and stretched. He moseyed over to the door and stepped outside. Thomas had free reign of the property, having been a family slave since he was twelve. Thomas walked down the path for five minutes. The two soldiers finished their grooming and entered the home.

"Massa, Massa, the Yankees are comin'!"

Thomas Jefferson ran at full speed, eyes wide open and sweat pouring from his brow. He burst into the house.

"Massa, I's just down the road. I ran into Jacob, the Patterson's young slave. He said we's all in danger. They's comin' this way . . . fast and mean."

Everyone in the house ran outside to look down the road. Everyone but Pauline. Pauline shimmied out the side window and slid along the perimeter of the house. While everyone looked out at the countryside, Pauline untied her saddle-less horse, threw herself over the animal's back and took off behind the house and barn to the open fields. While Pauline rode the horse without a saddle, the soldiers weren't prepared to do the same. She had a head start, knowledge of the land, and a chance to save herself from the noose.

Chapter Twenty-Four

A Message for Rosecrans

The sun rose in the east. Pauline traveled to the north. Another two miles or so, she'd be at a post office containing a spy drop-off. Could she save Rosecrans's troops before being re-arrested? Rosecrans frustrated Lincoln, Secretary of War Edwin Stanton, and General-in-Chief Henry Halleck. He spent time resupplying and building a training base instead of attacking Bragg and the Confederates. If Rosecrans continued to sit, he'd play into Bragg's hands through the raid of Colonel Starnes. If Pauline couldn't get the message to Rosecrans before he left his troops, thousands of Union men might die.

Pauline stopped on the crest of a hill. She looked in the direction she had come. She saw movement along the far away trail. She couldn't be sure, but she had to believe the Confederate soldiers were in hot pursuit.

The Post Office could be seen in the distance. She never wrote anything until just before delivery, because of Truesdail's warnings, but now the Post Office was in sight. So were the three soldiers. Pauline pulled sharply around the corner of the building, jumped off Banjo, and slapped the horse on his buttocks. Banjo seemed to understand the meaning, and continued at a gallop away from the Post Office. The soldiers turned the corner, saw the horse running in the distance and continued after the horse.

As soon as they passed by, Pauline scribbled her notes on the top of a barrel, found the secret opening of the spy drop and stuffed her life-saving message into the hole.

She had no hiding place and no one in sight except the soldiers chasing her horse. She had to get away from the Post Office so they didn't suspect she had hidden some note.

There was no place in fifty yards to conceal herself. The next best thing – Pauline ran as far away from the Post Office as she could and threw herself on the ground. She muddied up her right leg and tore the right side of her dress. She lay pretending to be unconscious.

The Rebs spotted her horse without its rider as soon as they had gained some ground. Realizing their prey was behind them, they turned on their mounts and came upon the prostrate Pauline in full actress mode, playing possum.

"Lady, y'all shown your true colors by running away from us. I don't know much about the spy business, but you sure act like a spy. This time we're going to tether you to your horse and deliver y'all to General Forrest. He can deal with y'all, and we'll be happy to have y'all out of our sight."

The Lieutenant jumped off his horse and knelt at the seemingly knocked out Pauline. He lifted her by placing his two hands on her arms and lifting her limp body to a sitting position. Pauline let out with a horrendous squeal.

"Oh, Mercy, my ankle is broken." She straightened out her left leg and screamed once again.

The Lieutenant stretched his grip, but did not let go of her arms.

"Oh, Lieutenant Pity me. I need to see my brother. Your stopping me from my journey is just like those Yanks who kicked me off of the stage and out of Louisville. This war's so cruel. It keeps family from family and man from wife. All I want is to find my brother...can't you please help me?"

"This here's a mighty fine performance Miss Cushman, and maybe I'm wrong. If I am I'll seek y'all out to give you an apology, but I think you're up to no good, and I'm going to let General Forrest make the call."

The ploy worked. The Lieutenant thought she fell off her horse, not that she dismounted to hide a note. Pauline may have been caught, but not before she put her information in the spy channel. Her acting skills probably saved the day for Rosecrans and his men.

Pauline wrote to me, *in war you win or lose, live or die, and the difference is often just a blink of the eye.*

Chapter Twenty-Five

The Fate of the Copperheads

Pauline later told me Truesdail and his officers felt an urgency about ending the war soon. While the war raged on in Tennessee, other parts of the country clamored for peace. Ohio, free from battlefield encounters, wanted the war to stop. Clement Vallandigham, a member of the House of Representatives, claimed we fought an illegal war and Lincoln violated the constitution.

To stop this movement, Union General Ambrose Burnside issued General Order Number 38 on April 13, 1863. The order made it illegal to criticize the war in the Department of the Ohio.

"Hereafter all persons found within our lines who commit acts for the benefit of the enemies of our country, will be tried as spies or traitors, and, if convicted, will suffer death. This order includes the following classes of persons . . ."

The order continued to state:

"The habit of declaring sympathies for the enemy will no longer be tolerated in the department. Persons committing such offences will be at once arrested, with a view to being tried as above stated, or sent beyond our lines into the lines of their friends."

Clement Vallandigham spearheaded the Copperhead movement.

A popular ditty of the time went as follows:

O, brothers, don't forget the time When Burnside was our fate,
And laws superseded By order 38.
Then like a free-born western man, Our Val spoke bold and true,
O, when he's chosen governor What will poor Burnside do.
Won't he skedaddle, As he's well used to do.

We weren't living in a democracy while we were at war. President Lincoln declared martial law. In the first months of the war, Lincoln took sweeping power suspending rights of American citizens. The right to privacy, free speech, and habeas corpus were all suspended by Lincoln's order.

On May 5, 1863, while Pauline risked her life to win the war deep in the South, the Union Army arrested Vallandigham as a violator of General Order Number 38. A court martial tried him on May 6 and 7. The Military Commission charged him with showing sympathy for those in arms against the Government of the United States.

They convicted and sentenced him to confinement in a military prison "during the continuance of the war" at Fort Warren.

On May 19, 1863, President Lincoln ordered Vallandigham deported and sent to the Confederacy.

Chapter Twenty-Six

Pauline's Charm Saves the Day

Back on the fields of battle Pauline gathered information against the enemy from a new source. The Lieutenant took his saddle off and directed one of the soldiers to tie it on the soldier's horse for travel.

Pauline sat in front of the Lieutenant as they rode his horse bareback across the countryside. During the ride, Pauline laid her head on the young Lieutenant's shoulder, placed her left arm around his back and her right hand stroking his chest.

Mile after mile she gently caressed the young man. By the time they arrived at the outpost the Lieutenant's hostile attitude was gone.

"Let me see if I can find y'all's brother, Miss Pauline."

Pauline had regained her part. She began looking for the fictitious brother Asa once more, and the Rebs were going to help her view Bragg's troop positions during her search.

After a few days of inquiries with her former captors, the Lieutenant turned her over to another set of escorts.

Junior officer after junior officer became her protectors as she traveled all around Bragg's fortifications. She gathered a treasure trove of information on how Bragg's forces were deployed and through a series of message handoffs the information eventually reached Truesdail.

Pauline seemed to star on a new stage.

Chapter Twenty-Seven

Shelbyville and the Military Engineer

Pauline arrived in Shelbyville, Bragg's headquarters, and stayed at the Evans House in the center of town. Pauline loved to play cards and drink mint juleps. Ralph Brunton, a military engineer, was also a guest. Pauline played Euchre, her favorite card game. She taught Ralph how to play and how to gamble.

"Miss Pauline you love this game. I'd love it more if I won the game more."

"Ralph, if you watched your cards the way you watch me, you'd play a better game."

"If I have to choose between looking and winning, I'll pick looking." Thursday night was quiet in the boarding house. Everyone went to bed except for Pauline and Ralph.

"Pauline, why don't you come to my room? We can have another drink and I can look at you closer than I can playing cards."

Ralph was a giant of a man. He stood well over six feet tall and weighed two hundred fifty pounds or more. He might have been a little fat, but he was mostly big and muscular."

"Sure, I'd love to. Ralph, how did such a big guy wind up making his living drawing designs on paper?"

"My Dad was a soldier in the war of 1812. He was a military engineer. He taught me how to draw fortifications and design pontoon bridges for river crossings early on. I loved it when as a kid; I didn't change my mind when I got big."

Pauline and Ralph went to Ralph's room. Pauline could drink a lot. Pauline saw Ralph's drawings on his table and asked about them.

"I'm gonna' present them to General Bragg tomorrow. He asked me to stage some defenses to keep Rosecrans from his doors."

"I'm impressed you work for the top guy around here."

"I'm impressed you finally came to my room." Pauline went to the giant man who sat at the drawing table and gave him a kiss.

"Let me pour you another drink and see where this takes us," Pauline said.

Pauline poured her trusty potion she used to spike Sam Davis' drinks. The potion had the same effect on Ralph. Long before he had a chance to be amorous, he fell into a deep stupor.

Pauline studied the drawings. What a find. Rosecrans could defeat Bragg if he knew how the defensive trenches, bulwarks and breastworks were placed. Pauline copied the drawings in great detail. She made drawings on the front and back of three sheets of paper. Never before had she made a note or drawing except moments before she dropped the writing into the spy network system.

Colonel Moore and Colonel Truesdail warned me about putting this stuff in writing. But this risk makes my actions significant to my country.

Chapter Twenty-Eight

Bolting With the Plans

The next morning Ralph woke up with a splitting headache and an empty bed. He came to the dining room hoping to find Pauline. The landlady said Pauline ate breakfast and left very early in the morning.

Before leaving, Pauline read an article in the newspaper, *The Union Army in Franklin hanged two Confederate spies, and issued an order stating, "All persons found within our lines who commit acts for the benefit of the enemies of our country will be tried as spies or traitors, and, if convicted, will suffer death."* The Confederate Army would respond in kind. The consequence, should Cushman be caught now, would surely be death.

Pauline told me that after reading the article she felt afraid for her life for the first time. She'd be safer on the road. She left Shelbyville, bolting from town to town in a set of stolen boy's clothes, searching desperately for Union soldiers who could take her home. Along the way a message reached her offering a job at a theater in Richmond. A job back on the stage at this point seemed a safe haven from the close calls of the last several weeks. But first, she needed to get back to Nashville to get her luggage and stage wardrobe.

Without a pass from Bragg or help from the Union Army, she would have to sneak across the border. Pauline returned to Milam, the Confederate smuggler who had been so kind to her at the start of her mission.

"Miss Cushman, you've been talked about since your last visit to this home," Mrs. Milam said. "The officers at the outpost say you have often traveled the South without an escort." The lady who had been so happy to have a celebrity as a house guest, spoke to Pauline in icy tones.

Benjamin Milam came to the door. "Madam, your presence puts my work in danger. I'm afraid you're no longer welcome here." With that, Mrs. Milam shut the door. No escort, no pass and no safe harbor.

She mounted Banjo and traveled down the rural road. In two miles she found the house of Mr. and Mrs. Bennington.

Pauline sat and sobbed on her horse. Nowhere to go—and death looming close behind her. She had real tears when she asked refuge for the night.

The Benningtons gave her shelter but it didn't last long.

Milam called on the local Confederate outpost and reported her escort-less wanderings. She hadn't been there an hour when four Confederate soldiers appeared at the door. They arrested her and brought her to the outpost of General John Hunt Morgan, second in command to General Forrest.

Chapter Twenty-Nine

John Hunt Morgan

"Oh my, did my sister like the sight of John Hunt Morgan." Her instructions were to be as demure as possible in getting information from the enemy. Pauline met men with a demure demeanor except when men indicated they were vulnerable to her charms. She had long ago decided she'd do anything for her country, if that anything included hanging so be it. If that anything included having sex with an enemy to gain an advantage for her country, so be it.

The bigger moral question, she thought, was not how she used her body for her beliefs, but how she used her mind to stop the abomination that was slavery in her beloved land.

Her letter to me was filled with happiness. She thought her duty just changed to a joyful flight of lust. She said John Hunt Morgan was a tall, muscular man with golden skin, ice blue eyes and a groomed beard. He had chiseled features, as if Michelangelo used a sculpting tool on his cheeks and jaw.

Morgan was a seasoned soldier, and proud of his ladies' man reputation. He earned the reputation because he oozed masculinity. He didn't care much for the feelings of any woman since his wife had died in complications of childbirth.

But . . . oh my, didn't John Hunt Morgan love the sight of my sister?

They both were secure in their own looks and their ability to draw the attention of the opposite sex. These two sexual athletes had met their match. Morgan's troops later spoke about the "smoke and fire" all around them when the General and the Lady lay together.

Morgan made Brigadier General in 1862. In 1863 the Confederate Congress praised him for his raids on the supply lines of General Rosecrans. When her latest escorts turned Pauline over to General Morgan, a new day dawned for Pauline and Morgan.

The relationship started out in a formal manner.

"Miss Cushman, You'll be in my custody until we reach General Forrest. It'll take several days to work our way to his outpost. Since no one has proven anything against you, I'll treat you with respect. Please don't give me a reason to treat you otherwise."

General Morgan stood by his horse as he spoke to Pauline. She had just dismounted. He invaded hr personal space, lowering his head to within inches of hers.

"Your celebrity will give you some consideration, but it'll also make you a huge example if you are tried and found guilty of treason." Pauline lost most of her limp developed when she feigned an injury and stood before her captor. Morgan was born in 1825, eight years before Pauline.

"Dear General Morgan, I'll cooperate in every way. I'm a loyal Southern lady whose object is to please you. You'll see I'm as anxious as you to win the war." He decided to let her recuperate by sharing his quarters with her. Pauline didn't object. Morgan was born in 1825, eight years before Pauline.

The next several days the Confederate troops under Morgan had some much needed rest. They started early enough in the morning, but shortly after noon, the march halted. Tents were set up and General Morgan watched over his prisoner. Over her was a descriptive phrase.

"John you are tireless. You're older than me; I'm the one who should have the energy."

The army cots provided in Morgan's command tent were thrown aside. Sleeping bags and quilts lay on the tent floor. The naked couple had a light sheet over them for some semblance of privacy.

Even command tents weren't very secure from prying eyes and tell-tale sounds.

"You arouse all the energy I've stored up on this lonely road," Morgan said.

"If I weren't accused of being a spy, would you want more of me than a few days in a tent?"

"If you were free to be a soldier's wife, I'd run from you. I lost my wife to childbirth. But I really lost her 'cause I was a soldier. She never knew when our goodbyes would be forever. It's awful on a wife and awful on a soldier."

"You're preaching to the choir, General Morgan. I was a soldier's wife." Pauline raised herself up on one elbow and pulled the sheet around her bosom.

"My husband played a banjo for a living. He died because of this war. My brother's in Bragg's command somewhere. He may be killed at any moment. You're going to kill me after you've used me enough."

The sun fell low in the western sky. The couple had been intimate for a few hours. The heat of the day made their bodies glisten. Their mixed perspiration filled the tent with the aroma of passion.

Morgan took Pauline in his arms and brought her back down to rest on the quilts, his face above her face.

"I've been with women, from nice ladies to camp followers. I'm using you like you're using me. I don't know if you're a spy or a patriot. I know you are heaven in my arms and this war is hell." Morgan lay on his back and pulled Pauline to rest on his chest. "If I can take you out of the madness by making love for a few hours it's good for you . . . good for me. I know I need you to be gentle."

Pauline couldn't believe Morgan showed his feelings. A first for her. But, she told me, he knew she needed to keep up her lies about her loyalty or hang.

"General Morgan, General Forrest is riding into camp. You better come out!" Morgan's aide de camp, Lieutenant James Cook, stood by the door of the tent. He spoke in as low a voice as possible.

"Thanks Jimmy. I'll be right out."

Both Morgan and Pauline stood, each grabbing their clothes and dressing with no conversation. Morgan left the tent while Pauline straightened up the bed sheets and quilts, folding them and placing them in a corner.

General Forrest waited for Morgan. Forrest was Morgan's direct superior. His subordinates respected and feared him.

He stood six feet two inches and 210 pounds. He stood over most men of his time. Forrest killed more than thirty enemy soldiers using his saber, pistol, and shotgun.

The week before he had a confrontation with Confederate Lieutenant Wills Gould. Forrest demoted the soldier during a heated argument. Wills shot Forrest in the hip. Forrest stabbed and sliced the man with his saber and killed him.

Outside of Morgan's tent, Forrest sat on his horse with his midsection wrapped in bandages to protect his wound.

"Good afternoon, General." Morgan said.

"Good afternoon yourself, Morgan. You have the celebrity in your tent?"

"I do sir. I've kept her secure. I'm taking her to your outpost."

"You don't have to keep her secure much longer. Did you compromise yourself John?"

"I haven't done anything to hurt my country or my army." Morgan feared no man. He found himself uncomfortable defending his actions in front of his mentor. Forrest was uncomfortable on his steed and angry about his wound. Forrest watched over Morgan's growth as an officer. He didn't want such a promising career to be damaged by foolish indiscretions.

"This pain is excruciating. I'm in need of a field hospital. My wound needs treatment for a few days and I don't want to deal with Miss Cushman while I'm recuperating."

Morgan stood at attention and saluted his superior officer. I won't disappoint you, General. I'll be at your outpost when you return from the hospital."

"Bring the woman to me at the outpost in a week, safe and secure. Bring her to me without compromising yourself, John. You have a reputation and a need. Don't forget the lady is probably a spy and you know things the enemy would love to know."

"I'll deliver her General. You'll have no cause to worry about my conduct."

The General ordered a wagon. Several soldiers helped Forrest off his horse, get in the wagon and make him as comfortable as possible for the painful trip ahead.

Morgan returned to Pauline. She dressed and sat reading a bible.

"You're with me for a few more days. I'll keep my distance if that's what you want."

"John, stop. You don't want to keep your distance from me, and you haven't any reason to think I want you to do so." Pauline closed the book and placed it on the field dresser.

"I loved my Charlie, but Charlie failed me. I suppose I failed him as well. I came to you willingly because our time is short and propriety be damned. There may be no proper tomorrow."

John lifted Pauline's hands with his, put her hands around his neck, and raised her up to his chest. Her feet came off the ground.

He said, "I don't know about love. I know about lust. I lust for you, for sure. I loved my wife, but we stopped being good for each other long before she died trying to give me a child. I know I have you now, I don't want to deal with tomorrows."

"John, I've been so lonely. Not alone. But lonely. I've longed for love . . . everyone does. Let's find some love, if just for today." Her words drifted softly like a ballad. His arms were tender as if they had no worries.

The couple talked about their hopes for a life after the war. Did he believe she was a spy? Did he care? But those questions had to remain unanswered. Forrest expected Morgan to bring the prisoner to him. Forrest wasn't a man to ignore. He was a violent man.

Morgan required respect himself. During the Murfreesboro Campaign he led a mounted division into Kentucky, from December 21, 1862, through January 1, 1863, against Rosecrans' supply lines. Congress promoted him to brigadier general for his bravery. Neither Forrest nor Morgan would disrespect the other.

Chapter Thirty

Nathan Bedford Forrest

General Morgan finally turned Pauline over to General Forrest. "Miss Cushman, I hope General Morgan treated you well while you were in his custody,"

"He did, General Forrest. But he didn't let me continue looking for my brother. I'm in hopes you'll see I am who I say I am. I hope to convince you I'm true to the Confederacy and you'll help me in my quest."

"Miss Cushman, I'm running a campaign that won't allow me to adequately verify your statement or prove you to be a spy. I'll make inquiry to see if you have caused immediate damage to my troops under General Morgan. If that's not the case, I'll see you are fairly treated at the hands of General Bragg."

"I'll cooperate in any inquiry. I'm anxious to begin."Pauline said.

"I'm still suffering somewhat from my wound and hospital stay. We'll start tomorrow morning," General Forrest said.

Pauline thought back to her training on the New York stage.

Don't ever come out of character during a performance. Always play your part while you can be seen, even off stage.

"If you examine me carefully, you'll find the bare truth."

And so she gave Forrest an invitation. The officers of the Confederacy weren't amoral men. They didn't walk from their code of honor whenever they were tested. But Pauline wasn't an ordinary test. There have been few women in history whose sexuality was so powerful the likes of Caesar and Marc Antony succumbed. Whether

Pauline was on Cleopatra's level could be argued, but that her beauty, carriage and personality acted as an aphrodisiac could not.

Forrest knew Morgan was smitten. His own resistance weakened. In the morning, Forrest interviewed Pauline in his tent. He interviewed her in his tent for the next three days. When he felt ready to get on a horse once again, he got off of his captured lady.

"Will you consider sending me back to Nashville? I know I haven't convinced you to help me find my brother, will you help me back to my home?"

"Pauline, I warned Morgan not to compromise himself when you placed him under your spell. I'm as much under your spell as he was . . . but I can't love my cause and release you. You'll charm the next man out of his senses."

Forrest, though captivated, determined to do his duty without waiver. Pauline wasn't saved, but she wasn't condemned yet either.

"Pauline if you're exonerated at the hands of Bragg, I'll see you are escorted 'til you find your brother. I suspect that won't be the case. I wish we would have more days together in our life. I hope you find a miracle. If it weren't for war, I wouldn't let you out of my life. I hope you can find a way home."

Forrest finished interviewing Pauline. He turned her over to General Bragg at Shelbyville.

Bragg hated most people. Especially Nathan Bedford Forrest and John Hunt Morgan. When Bragg learned Forrest and Hunt had a relationship with Pauline, she already sealed her fate. The charges were a formality. Bragg had men abused and shot for lesser offenses.

Chapter Thirty-One

Pauline's Contributions to the Union

To understand the magnitude of Pauline's contribution to the Union cause, you had to understand the great conflict among Confederate Generals. Joseph Johnston was the general in charge of the Western Division of the Confederate Army under President Jefferson Davis. His subordinate, General Braxton Bragg, was head of the Army of Tennessee. Bragg's second in command, General Nathan Bedford Forrest, was the chief cavalry officer and his second in command was General John Hunt Morgan, a cavalry officer.

General Joseph Johnston was the only one of that group who didn't have an intimate relationship with Pauline. Pauline gained information from the highest ranking officers of the Confederacy and did so even when caught in a web of jealousy.

Throughout his career Bragg fought almost as bitterly against his uncooperative subordinates as he did against the enemy. Subordinate officers made multiple attempts to have him replaced as army commander. I found these comments General Grant commented about the officers of both the Union and the Confederacy in his memoirs. He wrote: "Bragg ordered supplies from the quartermaster for his troops and quartermaster denied the request. But Bragg was, in fact, the quartermaster. Grant said, "Bragg had quarreled with every other officer in the army, and finally found a way to quarrel with himself!"

Pauline later explained the relationship each of her lovers had with the other officers. I'm going to list it as I remembered her descriptions: General Joseph Johnston: Johnston's relationship with

Jefferson Davis, President of the Confederacy rivaled Bragg's relationship. Bragg was a fellow soldier with Davis in the Mexican War. Joseph Johnston was Bragg's superior officer. President Davis feared Bragg alienated so many of his officers he'd have to be removed from command. Johnston came to Shelbyville to relieve Bragg, but found the troops in reasonably good spirits. Johnston left Bragg in command. He later regretted his decision. His final comments: "I know President Davis thinks he can do a great many things other men would hesitate to attempt. He tried to do what God failed to do. He tried to make a soldier of Braxton Bragg."

Nathan Bedford Forrest served under Bragg. Bragg berated Forrest as he did every officer who served under him. After much verbal abuse Forrest confronted Bragg in Bragg's field tent.

Forrest said, "I've stood your meanness as long as I intend to. You've played the part of a scoundrel, accusing me of not obeying your orders promptly. I dare you to do it, and I say to you if you ever again try to interfere with my command I'll slap your jaws and force you to challenge me. You may as well not issue any more orders to me, for I'll not obey them, and I will hold you personally responsible for any further indignities you endeavor to inflict upon me. If you threaten to arrest me or cross my path again it will be at the peril of your life." Bragg was intimidated. No wonder he wanted to humiliate Forrest if he had the opportunity.

John Hunt Morgan argued constantly with Bragg. Bragg would overrule Morgan's plans on a regular basis. Morgan's famous raid violated Bragg's direct order not to cross the Ohio River. The mutual distain caused by Bragg interfered with many opportunities for Confederate victories.

The three officers who dealt directly with Bragg knew best his shortcomings. They would have confined Pauline or sent her back to the North. When Bragg learned through his aides that Morgan and Forrest had been intimate with Pauline he needed to equal the conquest and then do what they wouldn't do . . . execute her.

Chapter Thirty-Two

Bragg's Treachery

Bragg commanded Pauline to sleep with him. Pauline willingly slept with Starnes and Forrest for tactical advantage. She bedded John Hunt Morgan because he attracted her immensely. But this . . .

"How could you find those men attractive? They're arrogant and ignorant," Bragg said as they lay in Bragg's huge bed. Bragg had taken over the largest home in Shelbyville for his residence.

"General, do you think I'm really free to make choices? Do you think if I objected to their advances I wouldn't be used for sex by them?" Pauline replied.

"My wife is far away and I'm lonely. You may be a spy but you are the prettiest woman I've ever seen. I hate those men, but I understand them wanting you."

"They were forced upon me by the necessities of war, General. You're so strong and forceful, how could I resist you after those experiences? I understand they're all jealous of you."

Pauline took her opportunity to flatter her captor. This was the man who would ultimately decide her fate.

"Pauline, I took you as a necessity of war. I'll always remember you. I've never made love like we have. If I wasn't a soldier, I'd find a way to have you with me," Bragg said.

He lay Pauline down once more. He waited for his physical enthusiasm to return and spent time indulging himself with his greatest fantasies.

"Are you thrilled by me Pauline?" Bragg asked.

"Of course. You know how good a lover you are. You know how exciting you are to me. Why do you need to hear me say it?" Pauline reached for a towel near the bed. She wiped bodily fluids from her skin and lay back next to the man who panted somewhat from his recent exertion.

"I want you to write letters to Morgan and Forrest about your love for me. I want you to tell them you never knew lovemaking until me. I want you to tell them they were nothing compared to me." "And if I write those letters what's in it for me? You plan on killing me if I'm tried and convicted," Pauline said.

"If you write those letters, I'll simply send you back across enemy lines. If you write those letters and leave, I won't take any further action. If you write those letters and I release you, and you return to the South, I'll have you shot on sight. No trials. No explanation."

"Of course I'll write those letters, Braxton. If you feel better about me because I showed loyalty to you, I'll write the letters willingly." Bragg rose from the bed and dressed. Pauline took that as a signal for her to do the same.

"I have pen and paper on the dining room table. I'm going to my office for the afternoon. Stay here under guard and write the letters. If I approve of the letters, and only if I approve, I'll keep my word to you."

Bragg dressed in his full uniform and brushed his hair in front of the dining room sideboard's mirror.

"Goodbye, Braxton, give me a kiss to inspire my writing."

Bragg turned to Pauline. He held her in his arms, reached back and squeezed her backside and gave her a soulful kiss.

"Braxton, why do you need the affirmation? Can't I just love you and stay by your side?" Pauline asked.

"You don't know the depth of my hate for those men. It doesn't even have to do with you, really. I want to hurt them and humiliate them in any way I can," Bragg said.

The Lady was a Spy

He let Pauline go, strutted to the front door and turned to face her.

"Remember, I need those letters to humiliate them when they read them. Make sure you write them strong enough for me to let you go."

"Kiss me once more before you go." Pauline said.

"I'll do the kissing after I read the letters." he said.

Bragg gave a final tug of his uniform coat, grabbed the door handle and swung the door wide open for a grand exit.

Pauline went to the bedroom and dressed in her best blouse and skirt. Bragg let her have some clothes in a closet in return for her voluntarily sharing his four poster. She returned to the dining room, looked at herself in the mirror and sat to write her letters.

Pauline wrote to me. She said she couldn't help the North if she were hanged. Writing such letters would be a betrayal somewhat of her feelings but the men were still enemies of the Union and protecting the Union came before any other consideration.

She gave thought to writing the letters in such a way Morgan would know it was not truly from her heart. After reflection, she knew that if she made the letter less than emphatic Bragg wouldn't be satisfied. She also believed if the letter emphatically rebuked Morgan for Bragg, Morgan would realize Bragg had coerced the letter.

She started, *Dear General Morgan* . . . After she finished the two letters, she laid them on the dining room table, went out to the garden and picked a fresh bouquet of flowers and placed them on the table next to the letters. She went to the closet where Bragg kept his whiskey and wines and found a bottle of champagne. She washed champagne flutes and plated crackers. Pauline went back to the bedroom, freshened her makeup and spritzed herself with perfume. Bragg returned just before dinnertime.

"The letters are prepared for your approval, and the table set for a toast," Pauline said.

"Let me see your letters," Bragg said. He took both of them to his rocking chair, sat and read each of them slowly, and carefully.

"The letters are fine, Pauline. You sold those men out handsomely."

"I didn't sell them out; I simply touted how much I cared for you," she said.

"Pauline, you're an evil woman who will say anything to get her way." Bragg rose from the chair, walked over to Pauline standing by the dining room table, and gave her a rough possessive kiss and a rough possessive hug.

"Braxton, you don't need to be rough with me. I'm compliant in your arms," Pauline said.

"Well let's have some champagne and let's return to bed to prove how devoted you are to me."

The couple drank some wine and returned to the bedroom where Bragg had his fantasies fulfilled once more.

Morning came. Bragg awoke and dressed immediately. Pauline got out of bed and dressed.

"Braxton are you releasing me today?" Pauline asked.

"Yes. Let's take my buggy to headquarters where I will make arrangements for your release." Bragg said.

"You are a dear man, and I'll be forever grateful," Pauline said.

The couple took the buggy waiting for Bragg in front of his residence. The buggy took them to the military compound to Bragg's office. They entered the waiting room where Benjamin Milam and Jonah Blincoe were sitting.

"Good morning gentlemen," Bragg said.

"Good morning General, I came at your request," Milam said.

"Good morning General, nice to see you again. I haven't seen Pauline since she left Nashville. We were supposed to meet at the home of my Wartrace friend, but she never appeared," Blincoe said.

"Thank you, you know this lady?" Bragg asked.

"I do General, that's the famous Pauline Cushman," Milam said.

"Correct sir. You gentlemen will have the chance to tell us what you know of Miss Cushman at her trial," Bragg said.

"Trial?" Pauline screeched. "What are you talking about? You promised. You promised," Pauline said as she realized the falseness of the General's actions.

"Sergeant, you and Corporal Smith are to take Miss Cushman to Titus's jail until we call for her when court convenes," Bragg said.

"You thought you could come within my command, play your tricks about finding your lost brother and spy on my troop's positions? You thought you could betray my hospitality that allowed you to travel with my troops, sleep with my troop commanders and laugh at me and my army?"

"The court martial's going forward whether or not we shared a bed." This is war and war rules apply. Your conduct will be measured in our court martial and we will see who is laughing at whom when this is all over.

"If I am found guilty, what will you do with me?" Cushman asked Bragg.

"You know the fate of spies," said Bragg. "You'll be hanged."

Pauline fell back and touched her hand against the waiting room wall. "General, I don't think I'd look well dangling at the end of a rope. If I must die, I hope you'll allow me to choose the manner of my death."

"You will," Bragg repeated, "be hanged." Bragg motioned to the guards who took Pauline by either arm and escorted her out of the waiting room and around back to the jail building. The trial would start as soon as Bragg called all of the officers and witnesses together . . . before the day was over.

Chapter Thirty-Three

The Court Martial

A chill ran through General Braxton Bragg's office. Pauline was cold even though it was warm outside. The walls were covered with faded brocade, popular before the Union Army ravaged the South and most of the once-proud antebellum plantations. Two captains and a lieutenant, dressed in formal Confederate uniforms, sat behind a long table.

Milam appeared as a witness. Captain Mitchell Landreville, company Judge Advocate General, led the prosecution.

"Mr. Milam, how did you meet Miss Cushman?" he asked.

"Miss Cushman asked to stay at our family home right after leaving Nashville for a southern exploration," Milam said.

"Did you find her suspicious? Barnes asked.

"Yes. She had no luggage even though travelling to find her brother and stay with him. It seemed odd."

"Did you see her a second time?"

"I did. She returned to our house last month and sought help in reaching Nashville. She wanted me to smuggle her back without a pass."

"What did you do when she asked you to transport her?" Barnes asked.

"I refused to let her into our home. As soon as she left, I saddled up my horse and reported her to the Confederate outpost down the road from my home," Milam said.

"Thank you Mr. Milam. You may be excused," Landreville said.

Daniel Frye, a young lieutenant, also a JAG officer, stood and faced the military officers acting as judges.

"I have no questions of this witness," Frye stated to the court.

"The prosecution calls Mrs. Lorraine Hawthorne.

A large lady, shoulders straining at her blouse, rubbed her meaty fists together. She waddled to the witness stand and dropped her weight into the chair.

Captain Frye asked, "Your name is?"

"Mrs. Lorraine Hawthorne."

"Mrs. Hawthorne, what did you see when you stepped into Miss Cushman's guestroom?"

"I saw her sitting on the bed with her right leg crossed over her left, holding her shoe."

"What else did you see?" the soldier continued.

"She looked up at me and gasped. She had ripped off her heel and had a piece of paper stuffed in the hollow."

"What then?"

"I rushed to her side, ripped the paper from her and slapped her face." Mrs. Hawthorne swept her sledgehammer fist across her body as a description of her act.

"I knew she was up to something no-good, and she proved me right."

Mrs. Hawthorne reached behind her head and adjusted her untidy chignon.

"Is this the paper you took from her?"

"Yes," she said. "It's a drawing of General Bragg's fortifications. I clean for the General. The military engineer, Ralph Brunton, brought these to the General's office a few days ago. I caught 'Miss Actress' lady with copies of the plans."

"Where were you when you saw her that day?"

"Everybody made a fuss over Miss Cushman. Colonel Johnson pranced, arm in arm with her, around the General's quarters. Because she's a famous actress, she's treated like a queen." Mrs. Hawthorne spitted somewhat as she speeded up her testimony.

"The men were falling all over her while Colonel Johnson showed off. I scrubbed the floor of the bathroom. I peeked my head out and saw Miss Cushman slip away from the Colonel. She lifted up the drawings, turned them over twice, and then ran back to where the Colonel had been."

Hawthorne put her hands on the rungs of the chair and lifted her hulk up from the seat for a moment. After squeezing back between the rungs, she continued.

"I figured she had an eyeful and I thought those drawings were none of her business. I decided to find out just why she was so friendly with the officers and so nosy besides."

The three officers acting as judges took notes. As they listened to the Hawthorne testimony, they each eyed the defendant. Pauline sat as if posing for a portrait. Her hair fell in ringlets around her golden complexion. Her eyes stared away from the people involved in deciding her fate. Even General Bragg, the man who had used her and condemned her, couldn't help sneaking admiring glances at the statuesque maiden.

Pauline remembered how cold she was.

"Guilty" the first officer said. "Guilty" followed the second, then the third.

General Bragg stood, turned to the beautiful woman about to be sentenced, and said, "Miss Pauline Cushman, the lady the South revered for your heroism on behalf of the Confederacy, I find you betrayed your country and your countrymen."

Pauline turned and looked directly into the eyes of General Bragg.

The General said, "You came to me as commander of your lost brother's brigade to enlist my help. You took my hospitality in making your search to find your brother among my troops and used the occasion to spy on our country." The General's face became flushed. He bit out his words in what seemed to be controlled rage.

"You won't have a chance to turn on those who admired you again. You'll be hanged by your neck until dead. The sentence will be executed within the week in the Fort's public square."

Pauline had no response. She froze. Her ears rang; her mouth felt full of cotton. She didn't cry because her tear ducts dried up. Her heartbeats belied her body's stillness. They thumped loud enough to fill her ringing ears. She finally spoke.

"You've made a mistake General Bragg. You're condemning an innocent woman and betraying your honor as a man in the same cowardly moment. I'll answer to my God on judgment day, but you'll rue the day you turned on those who trusted you and be damned by God on judgment day for your betrayal . . . MAY YOU BE DAMNED, SIR."

Chapter Thirty-Four

Titus and the Jail

Two soldiers marched from the back of the room. Each took an arm and walked on either side of Pauline. They removed her from the courtroom and escorted her to the military jailhouse on base. The jailer, Titus Wilson, opened the door to the watch room at the front of the building made from slab timber.

"Howdy, Titus. Where do you want your prisoner?" One of the soldiers asked.

"Howdy, Jethro. Put her in the first cell so I can keep an eye on her." Titus unlocked the door to the cellblock so the soldiers and their prisoner could enter. The two soldiers placed Pauline inside the cell, shut the door and invited Titus to turn the key in the lock. Titus took the large key from his back pocket, turned it in the lock and walked out of the cellblock with the two guards.

Darkness.

The sun had already set when she walked into her cell. The jailer stayed in the adjoining room. Pauline was alone.

Pauline fell on her knees. "My God, my God, why have you forsaken me?" The trial and conviction of Jesus, the truly innocent one came racing to her mind.

"Lord I so wanted to make a difference. I didn't want one man to own another; I didn't want one man to beat another." Pauline stood. "Why did I give up my reputation as an actress? For this? Why did I listen to Moore and Truesdail, to be hung?"

Pauline stood and placed her hands on the rusty, musty, greasy bars of her cell. "How did I go from a tomboy kid in Michigan to this?" She paced from one end of the cell to the cot and back.

"I slept with men for the good of my country. Was I just a camp follower? You gave your whole life for us; couldn't I give my body in sacrifice to something bigger than me?"

Sounds came from the jail office. Clanking of tins and muffled conversations mingled with the smell of beans and rice.

"Lord I lied every day in pursuit of justice. I thought my country would see how a poor Creole kid could be a heroine. Now I'm going to die. No hero. No honor." Pauline fell silent. Her eyes filled and overflowed with tears. "Damn. I don't want to cry."

Her hands trembled and her head ached. Hammers seemed to be pounding on her body. She took off her shoes, loosened her dress and lay face down on the cot. She didn't think she could sleep, but when she awoke the sun started to shine in the cell window. A tin tray with yesterday's food lay at the base of her cot. She smelled a faint odor of rancid bacon. Pauline felt the sun shine on her face. She smiled. The rays were warm and comforting. Pauline thought, *I'm not quitting. I've given too much to go meekly like a sheep. I know they'll hang a woman. There will be a lot of outcry, but it's war. Will they kill a sick woman? A deathly sick woman?*

"Hey Mr. Jailer, you have any coffee for your only prisoner?"

What will the public think about that cruelty? A good many Southerners can't believe the darling who toasted the Confederacy at a risk to her life would be a spy. I think I'm going to get deathly sick when it comes time for my execution.

Chapter Thirty-Five

Pauline's Stay in Jail

"Morning," Titus, the lanky jailer, drawled. "I've got some coffee for y'all, but nothin' more." He shuffled sideways like a crab skittering over water until he reached Pauline's cell. He held a mug of hot coffee and passed in between the rusted gray bars.

"Miss Cushman, y'all are my guest for a few days 'til they stretch your neck. There's no stage here for you to do your actin', just a cot and a chamber pot."

Cushman sipped the hot coffee and gave the soldier a small curtsey, and a slight smile. Maddie, the cleaning lady, mopped the floor outside the cells. When Titus spoke she moved to the corner of the room with her mop in hand. Pauline smoothed her taffeta dress with her hands and sat on her cot as if it were a ballroom chair.

Pauline thought Titus looked to be in his mid-twenties. He had hair the color of chestnuts and wore it longer than they'd allow in most eastern posts. He dragged his left leg slightly as he walked from coffee pot to cell door.

Pauline fascinated Maddie. When Titus went outside she struck up a conversation. "What do you think of your jailer Miss Cushman? That Titus, he sure is a good lookin' soul. A little rough around the edges, but he'd do anything for you."

"He looks a lot more warrior than jailer." Pauline said. She noticed the shirt around Titus' shoulders tightened when he moved, stretching over shoulders almost too large for the man's waist.

"The boys in sick bay tell me Yankees shot him off his horse in the battle of Shiloh. His commander's letting him sit out a few battles," Beverly said.

"How'd he get off of the battle field?" Pauline asked.

"His horse, Romeo, tripped when they shot Titus, but waited 'til the soldier could slide back in the saddle. They say man and horse have been inseparable since then."

"So where's his horse?" Pauline asked.

"Who, Romeo? He's tied up out back. Titus goes out to see him every so often during the day," Maddie said. Pauline seemed to enjoy the conversation of a woman, and continued.

"Do you have any children?"

"I do ma'am. I have two daughters and a son. They're the pride of my life. My husband's too old to be at war, but he is sure good to me."

"You and Titus get along?" Pauline said.

"Sure. He's just a young'un, but a decent sort." Titus came back inside.

Pauline turned to him."Titus, they're all wrong about me . . . I'm loyal to the South and partial to Southern gentlemen."

"I don't know nothin' about trials ma'am. I'm just doin' my time for Tennessee, my folks and my horse."

Titus got up from his chair by the window and shuffled a little closer to the cell.

"I recon if the General says you're a traitor, you're a traitor."

"Did you ever hear of me before today?"

"Sure . . . everybody knows you toasted ole' Jeff Davis, and they kicked you out of the theatre."

"I sure did. I toasted our President and the South from that Yankee stage. I grew up in New Orleans and always fancied our Southern boys. Southern boys like you, Titus."

"Yeah, that's right," Maddie added. "I read how the theatre manager fired you and they ran you out of Yankee territory and across Southern lines."

Maddie swung her mop pretending to be at work and not just part of the conversation.

"Does Mrs. Hawthorne, the lady who testified against me, like our Southern gentlemen?" Pauline loosened the buttons on the neck of her formal dress to reveal her ample cleavage.

"No, ma'am she don't take kindly to us fellows, and I can't say we're drawn to her much. She probably could beat on us pretty bad if she had a mind to."

"Well she's hurt me. She's hurt me bad. She doesn't like actresses or pretty women."

Pauline warmed to the conversation. Now that she had Titus in close range she stood up near the cell door and gave Titus some body language that would please a man.

"She made up that story about my hiding secret plans so she could be a star in the eyes of her beloved General Bragg and stop him gawking at me all the time. She's a hateful woman."

Maddie didn't bother mopping. She said, "That Hawthorne lady gave me a shove the other day when I cleaned the porch on General Bragg's office. She thinks she's the only one who can clean for the General. I thought she'd break me in half when she pushed me up against the porch door and kicked my mop bucket."

Maddie, dressed in a dull tan cotton dress with a threadbare grey apron, pushed her hair from her round pudgy face and sat on a cell cot.

Titus clutched a bar on the cell with his left hand and held his tin coffee cup with his right.

"You ain't the first to tell of Hawthorne's horrors. They say she has as foul a temper as the General hisself," Titus said.

"You hush, now Titus. If the General hears you, you'll have to come in here and be a prisoner with me," Pauline said.

She looked directly into Titus's eyes, moved her bosom to and fro and said, "I'd sure like your company, but who'd take care of Romeo?"

Maddie stood up, shook her head, took her mop and bucket and walked to the next cell.

"You sure sound like an easy lady to me. They say actresses are hussies', they may just be right."

"Oh, Maddie, I'm just occupying my time. Even if Titus would give me some attention, I'll be dead and gone in a week. You'll have forty more years to be with a man. You can't begrudge me a few moments of flirtation?"

Maddie looked full on to Pauline. "You know, you're right. I didn't think about how short a time you have and how lucky I'm goin' to be when this war is over. I'm fixin' to clean out back and let you do your carrying on." Maddie put her mop in the bucket, picked up the bucket and shuffled out of the cell.

When she opened the door to the back room, she slung her bucket to the other side of the door, spilling some water on the floor, and shut the door behind her. Pauline unbuttoned two more bodice clasps and moved up tight to the bars to give Titus a full view of her golden skin.

"Titus, it's so cold in here. Do you have a blanket you could put around me?"

"Ma'am, you're still a prisoner, as much as I'd like to put a blanket around you, I'm your jailer. I'm leaving you cold and I'm keepin' myself safe from your charms."

Pauline fell faint to the floor. Titus shook his head, opened the cell, picked the unconscious lady from the floor and placed her on the cot. Titus couldn't revive her. After smelling salts were opened and she only jerked her head a little, Titus locked the cell, left the jail and reported her medical condition to Bragg's aide, Captain George Meyer.

Chapter Thirty-Six

Bragg and Johnston

"Good morning, General, what brings you to my door?"

"Good morning Braxton, I came to see what you needed for the upcoming battle."

Joe Johnston pulled up a chair and sat in front of his subordinate officer.

"I heard you have Miss Pauline Cushman in your guardhouse. After her toast to Jeff Davis, who thought she'd be a spy?"

"I trusted her. She traveled from town to town where I had regiments looking for her missing brother. It turns out she wrote down our positions and troop strengths. We caught her in the act or we'd still think of her as a daughter of the Confederacy."

"So you're going to hang her?" Johnston asked.

"I interrogated her myself. She's definitely a spy."

"So you're going to hang her?" Johnston prodded Bragg.

"She came down sick. It's bad enough to hang a woman, but a sick woman being hanged would bring too much flack." Bragg tugged on his wool uniform coat and continued. "I've got too many enemies in the Army to make myself an easier target than I am." Johnston stood up and poured coffee from an urn on Bragg's desk.

"Where's your prisoner now?"

"I'm moving her to Doctor Blackman's house to be cured so I can hang her." General Bragg spread out Ralph Brunton's battle fortifications for Johnston's view.

"This is what we'll look like. Just leave me in command and I'll show Jeff Davis why he likes me," Bragg said.

"That's going to happen, Braxton, if the President takes my recommendation." Johnston took another look at Brunton's plans and continued.

"I'm going to recommend it. Don't make me sorry for it. President Davis wanted me to remove you from command if you were shaken because of Rosecran's attacks on you." Johnston swallowed the last bit of coffee from his mug. "I thought about it because you've had so many fights with your officers."

"You know they disrespect me," Bragg said.

General Johnston put his coffee mug down on Bragg's desk. "Braxton, you need to get your generals and colonels on the same page with you."

"I know, Joe, it's just that Morgan and Forrest are insubordinate most of the time." Bragg pulled at his britches. They were rubbing on his boils every time he took a step.

"I've given General Forrest and General Morgan a lesson or two in humility, but I still can't stand their smugness," Bragg said. Bragg rubbed his hands together, and then rubbed his hands on his hips and back to the desktop.

"Whenever I tell them my tactics, they think they know better. They make me dress them down in front of their men so my soldiers know who's running things."

Johnston said, "Braxton, rank doesn't confer privilege or give power. It imposes responsibility. You're in command, but you need to bring them around. You can't be fighting the enemy when you're fighting your own soldiers."

The sun broke through the uncovered windows streaming light on the pock marked face of Bragg.

"You're right, Joe. Rosecrans is always trying to break through my defenses. My arrogant underlings always taking potshots at my command decisions, and now I have a woman spy I need to hang, but she comes down sick."

Johnston responded. "I think you're right about the hanging. You'll be questioned by some about the court martial and the death sentence. If you hang a sick woman there'll be hell to pay."

"No wonder my feet hurt . . . everyone's stepping on my toes."

"Listen, your corps and division commanders have complained to President Davis. Hardee and Leonidas Polk asked Davis to put me in your place. Your division commander, Cheatham, vowed he wouldn't serve under you again." Johnston stood and pushed his chair back.

"Not only that, Braxton . . . Breckinridge wants to challenge you to a duel."

"That drunk . . . " Bragg said. "Look Joe, Breckinridge is supposed to handle the subordinates. He's been inept." Johnston reached over and put his hand on Bragg's shoulder.

"Sorry for your troubles, Braxton. I took the liberty of seeing your troops. They're in a lot better shape than most of the Confederate installations. You need to get a handle on your officers, but don't worry about the carping for now. I'm telling the President you have things in hand."

"Thanks Joe. I had to court martial Colonel McGowan, because he thought he knew better than me and wouldn't follow orders. I've been so attacked I thought about stepping down." Bragg shuffled his papers and stacked them in a neat pile. "Having your support makes it easier to carry on."

"You've got a battle to take care of. I'm heading back to Richmond and you're going to deal with Rosecrans and his Yankee darlings. Good Luck."

Johnston picked up his gloves and hat, waited for the obligatory salute from Bragg, returned it and sauntered out the door.

Bragg did have a battle to win. He had most of his troops protecting Guy Gap, the most likely road for Rosecrans to mount his attack. He stationed another platoon at Bell Buckle Gap. The rest of the platoons had to respond as needed.

That damned Pauline Cushman saw my plans. Lucky we caught her in time.

"I hope Pauline is well enough for me to hang her soon," Bragg said out loud but to no one in the room.

Chapter Thirty-Seven

Pauline Charms the Doctor

Bragg sent Pauline to Dr. Blackman's office to treat her sickness. He needed her hung soon. Soon enough to stop her spying and soon enough to keep his indiscretions quiet.

Dr. Blackman's house was plantation large. He had converted the front parlor to a medical office. Oriental carpets covered the large rooms.

"Come over to the examining table so I can look at you Miss Cushman. Your color is pale and you look as if you're anemic."

"I'm coming doctor. I'm moving slow and could use your gentlemanly assistance in getting on the table."

Pauline's forest green dress had Pagoda sleeves and a waist that accented her hour glass figure.

"I'll lift you after you remove your pantalets and chemise. I'll give you a moment." The good doctor left the room. Pauline removed her undergarments, leaving her dress on. She slipped her hand into the doctor's traveling bag and removed a scalpel. She placed the scalpel inside her underclothes and perched herself next to the table.

"I'm ready for you, Doctor," she said in her sweetest voice.

He walked to the examining table wearing a stethoscope in the new binaural design. Blackman lifted Pauline from her waist and placed her on the table. He put his hand on Pauline's forehead, asked her to open the bodice of her dress, and listened to her heartbeat.

Pauline touched the doctor's left hand and moved it to her right breast. "I seem to be having a pain in my nipple that won't go away."

"Open your bodice so I can examine the nipple." he said.

After he thoroughly examined one of the most admired breasts in the country, he examined her left breast with equal scrutiny.

"I don't find any abnormality, Pauline."

"Thank you doctor, could you please check my abdomen. I'm having an itching just below my navel." Dr. Blackman continued his examination. By the time he completed the examination Dr. Blackman fell under the spell Pauline placed on men who had the pleasure of such close contact.

Chapter Thirty-Eight

Bragg visits the Infirmary

Bragg continued his emotional roller coaster ride. He had graduated at the top of his class with his good friend, Confederate President Jefferson Davis. His reputation for fighting with every soldier, officer or infantryman, troubled his superiors. While he generally disliked the soldiers above and below him in command he showed compassion to the wounded. He made a weekly tour of the infirmary. Today Bragg met Colonel Grippo, the surgeon in charge. The Colonel held a clipboard with names of the wounded men in B ward. As they walked among the sick beds, the General spoke.

"How are you today soldier?"

"I'm doin' the best I can General. I'd sure like to have another leg so I could stand up from this bed and greet you proper."

"You've served your country well, soldier. We'll win this damned war so you can go home to your wife and family."

"Yes, Sir, General. Thank you General. God bless you sir."

Bragg took the clipboard and checked off the patient's name. He and the Colonel continued to the next bed.

"And how are you doing Lieutenant?" The General bent over to hear the wounded soldier.

The man's bandaged face covered his left eye then wound around his skull to his right ear. He raised himself slightly and drooled as he spoke. "I tried to get a message to you sir, when Rosecrans scouts tore me up." The soldier let his head back on the pillow after speaking.

"When did you see them?"

"Yesterday morning sir. They were checking out Bell Buckle Gap with two dozen cavalrymen. When I spotted 'em I turned my horse and galloped back toward headquarters. They shot me out of my saddle. Joe Buhler, the Johnny Reb in the next bed, spotted me and hauled me into safety."

The soldier put his head back on the pillow in exhaustion.

"He wouldn't of been shot if it weren't for me."Joe said.

He made a croaking sound slumped back and lost consciousness.

"Let's go Colonel; no one reported Rosecrans near the Bell Buckle Gap. Have my junior officers done me in again?" The General dropped the clipboard on the Surgeon's desk at the front of the hospital and marched back to his headquarters, Colonel Grippo jogged behind him.

Chapter Thirty-Nine

The Doctor Takes the Lady to Bed

"Dear Dr. Blackman, could you see me to my bed? I really am feeling quite faint."

Pauline still sat on the examining table. The good medical man seemed to salivate at the prospect of tucking the poor sick lady into his upstairs bed. An upstairs bed placed far away from any who might knock on his front door.

"Why certainly, dear, take my hand and I'll guide you upstairs. You can rest in my brand new Oxford brass bed."

Blackman took her arm, helped her rise and walked by the front door of the home.

"Wait just a moment while I turn the office sign to 'closed' and lock this door. That way no one will disturb us . . . I mean you, while you recuperate."

Pauline waited for the hand of her would-be lover and climbed the staircase in a faltering manner letting her escort help her with his hands around her back and lightly cupping her breast.

"I'll get you a robe, Pauline."

The actress sat on the bed and watched the doctor open his armoire. He took out a red silk robe with a gold cord belt.

"Won't you warm me in bed Doctor? I'm not long for this world and the warmth of a gentleman like you will be my last loving memory. I'll slip into the dressing room to freshen up a bit."

When Pauline entered the bedroom once more she found Dr.

Blackman in bed wearing nothing but a smile. Pauline, fully dressed, straddled the man in the bed so the bedcovers were tight around the man whose face flushed with anticipation.

"Do you see my right hand Dr. Blackman? It holds your very sharp scalpel. If you move a whisker, I'll slit your throat like a stuck pig." Blackman's eyes changed from dewy to hyperthyroid. Pauline raised herself while still straddling Blackman.

"Kindly place your arms above your head and clasp your fingers together."

Pauline placed the scalpel on the doctor's jugular vein, so the man moved very gently as he did her bidding. She slid her body up beneath the man's armpits with the full weight of her body on his chest.

"I'm going to tie your hands to your nice new Oxford brass bed with your lovely gold cord."

"I meant you no harm Pauline, don't hurt me."

"I won't hurt you Dr. Blackman, if you don't fight me. I'm going to tie your hands and tuck you tight enough so you can't work yourself out of the bed."

She doubled the cord around his wrists and secured him to the bed. Pauline jumped off of the bed, and tucked the blankets tight on either side.

"You can tell them I tied you up when you were sleeping. If you tell them any earlier than tomorrow morning, they'll know you shouldn't have been in bed . . . certainly not with a Yankee spy! They'll hang you next to me. Just to help you in your explanation, I'm stuffing your sock in your mouth. I took the liberty of borrowing one of your bandages to wrap around your head."

She tightened the bed covers so tight thrashing would be impossible, and then left her caretaker to his own care.

Chapter Forty

The Tullahoma Campaign

June 1863

Bragg's boils were so inflamed he couldn't ride out with his men to confront Rosecrans.

We'll lead the Yankees right down Bell Buckle Pass and into our ambush . . . We'll jam the pass once Rosecrans' lightening brigade rushes through, he thought.

***

Rosecrans moved his men. Lincoln's tiresome lectures prodding him to attack are over.

My men are finally ready and Bragg's men are worn and ragged.

Rosecrans sent a few troops into Bell Buckle Gap to fool Bragg about his intentions.

The battle raged on. Soldiers in Blue drove into the gaps not protected by Bragg's men. Young men in Gray were killed in large numbers that day.

Chapter Forty-One

Titus Gets his Wish

While the battle raged, Titus watched over the military jail and his very fast horse.

"Titus, don't you look handsome this afternoon." Pauline had slipped through back passages from the doctor's house to the military jail.

"Pauline, what are you doin' here? You're supposed to be too sick to be hung and sure too sick to be walking around."

Pauline stood in the open door of the guard's office. She shut the door and walked up to Titus so close her lips almost touched his face.

"I'm deathly sick Titus. Doctor Blackman said I wouldn't live to be hung. He said he wanted to let me taste love once more before I died, but his age stopped him from helping me. I begged him to let me come to you."

"What do you mean come to me? I'm just a soldier, what can I do to help you?"

"Titus, you're big and strong, you can't tell me you're not smart enough to know when a woman wants to take you to bed, or take you to a jail cell bunk if that's all she has."

Titus had just made a fresh pot of coffee. He sipped the hot brew as she opened the door. He put down his coffee mug and put his hand on Pauline's shoulder.

"You know I like . . . " Pauline reached her hand around Titus' neck and pulled his lips to hers. He started to pull away but he couldn't. The man who had been living alone in a jail for weeks and before that with hundreds of men in the field reacted. Titus took Pauline's head in his long hands, placed his lips back on hers in a position that allowed him to dwell in and around her mouth for minutes.

Pauline placed her hands around Titus' butt and pulled him into her. He needed no further encouragement. Pauline took off her dress and shoes and let them fall to the floor. An afternoon rain pattered lightly on the jail's tin roof. They made their way through a cell door and lay on the bunk bed remade just this morning. The sheets were starchy and fresh from being hung outdoors.

Titus rose to the occasion and made love to Pauline as only a pent-up and deprived twenty-something soldier could hope for.

Pauline, who knew how to use her feminine charms to her advantage, applied herself with an uncontrived enthusiasm.

When Titus thought he finished lovemaking, Pauline used her feminine skills to arouse him once more. He eventually obliged. Titus turned on his back as Pauline administered a long soothing back rub that made the young man doze off for a bit. As the rain continued with a soothing white noise the man went back to being a pampered boy.

Pauline's movements, however, were quick and silent. By the time Titus noticed the back rub stopped, Pauline vacated the cell, underwear in one hand, cell key in the other.

"Titus you are a nice young man and a very good lover. If you weren't I wouldn't have waited for a second time before leaving you." She threw her underclothes, dress and shoes in a feedbag.

Pauline had picked up her clothes and Titus' uniform. Pauline rolled up the sleeves and pant legs of the big uniform so she could move in the outfit.

"I'm taking your clothes and your horse so I can save my life. If I'm successful, it's because you let me live. If I'm not successful, you made me a happy woman twice before I died."

Chapter Forty-Two

A Spy once More

Pauline opened the door to the back room and peeked out the back to see if she had a clear moment to grab the horse. Romeo grazed on a long tether behind the guardhouse. The rain subsided. Pauline untied the tether and rode the horse without a saddle. Pauline leaned close to the fast Romeo's ear.

"Come on, you mighty horse, save me now like you saved your master."

Romeo dipped his head twice, turned to see his rider from the corner of his eye and started a swift gait through the back of the prison compound to an open field.

Pauline was sick. She feigned her sickness to gain time but Mother Nature helped her performance. She picked up an ailment that would keep her weak for months to come.

Pauline whispered in Romeo's ear again. "Let's go pal . . . to the spy drop. I drew new plans at Dr. Blackman's house."

Pauline found a post office eight miles from Bragg's headquarters and placed the plans in the designated vessel.

If I die now, my death won't be in vain.

Chapter Forty-Three

Shelbyville to the Duck River Bridge

Bragg had other things on his mind besides the talented actress he let into his bed before condemning her. The Tullahoma campaign raged on until July 3rd. He called in Forrest and Morgan to discuss the battle situation.

"What did your scouts find out?" Bragg asked.

"Rosecrans continues to hold the passes, so we can't get food or supplies from the standard routes," Forrest replied.

"And your men can't open one of them?" Forrest stared at Bragg for seconds before answering.

He spit on the ground and said, "The Yankees have the new repeating Spencers that beat our three-banded Enfields every time." Bragg returned Forrest's stare with a sneer of his own.

"And so we can't eat or re-supply our ammunition?"

"Rosecrans' troops seem to know our defensive positions. They attack every place we aren't," Morgan chimed in.

"Let Forrest tell me why he can't open our lines." Bragg snapped at Morgan.

Morgan stepped toward Bragg in reaction to the remark, but stepped back again in silence.

"It looks like someone got your battle plans, General. How'd you think that happened?" Forrest asked.

"You should've taken care of that spy before you brought her to me, Bedford."

"She and the plans were with you the time last I saw her, Braxton." Forrest pulled a letter from inside his uniform jacket, and shoved it back in.

"And it seems you were with her a lot more than any of us," Forrest said.

While Rosecrans used Pauline's stolen plans to rout Bragg, Truesdail tried to save Pauline from the hangman's noose. He sent ninety scouts to search for her. Pauline hid on the outskirts of Shelbyville. A battle raged. She hid in a stand of trees near the Duck River Bridge.

The Confederate troopers retreated to the railroad depot. Dozens of soldiers, Blue and Gray, died in the volley.

The Union forces from the 3rd Regiment Indiana Cavalry appeared out of the side streets and engaged the enemy with small arms and sabers. The Confederate soldiers had three cannons. Yankees drove them away using pistols. Pauline recognized one of General Forrest's leaders, General Wheeler, leading his men.

Wheeler tried to retake the Duck River Bridge near Pauline's hiding place. The 1st Confederate Cavalry charged across the bridge only to find they were outnumbered by the Union cavalry on the other side. The mass of men and horses all rushed for the bridge. Men were trampled underfoot and killed . . . many plunged into the stream and drowned, others were shot while swimming. General Wheeler narrowly escaped by swimming down river. Pauline saw him throw his saber away so he could swim towards the river bank.

This second retreat from Shelbyville became a race to get away. The fighting moved on. Pauline held Romeo by his reins as she hid standing next to an oak tree. Could she mount Romeo and make a run for it? She couldn't be captured again. From the other side of the tree stand six men dressed in civilian clothes were on foot holding their horses just like Pauline. They circled her.

Oh no, not again. Not when I finally broke free, she thought.

"Stand and identify yourself, soldier." The leaders of the band of men were brothers, Captain Eric Black and Lieutenant Chris Black, two of Truesdail's best. They were some of Pauline's trainers back in Nashville.

Eric came up to Pauline, who then recognized him. "Oh, my God, Eric."

Pauline threw her arms around her friend and sobbed. She placed her head in Eric's chest and shook for several moments.

"I've prayed for this moment ever since they caught me. I thought I was lost . . . now I'm so glad I'm found." Pauline straightened up, kissed Eric on the cheek and turned to the other men in the party.

"Okay guys, take me home." Pauline sighed.

The six men were part of the ninety scouts looking for Pauline. She wore Titus' Confederate Uniform.

"Come on Pauline. We have lots of people waiting to thank you for your work. Let's take you to Nashville and some champagne," Eric said. The group crossed over the Union lines of attack and made it back to Nashville without incident.

Rosecrans captured the territory holding Pauline. While the Union chased her Confederate executioners from their gallows, Pauline's information proved vital to the Union soldiers' victory.

God helps those who help themselves she thought, as she saw the city limits of Nashville once again.

The war paused for a day in Nashville. Pauline's espionage days were over. Her celebrity as a spy meant she could never again work behind enemy lines. However, her actions made her the newest national hero for the Union. Truesdail asked General James Garfield, head of the Nashville forces, if he would provide troops to celebrate her victories and escape.

General Garfield personally led a troop of Cavalry to salute Pauline in front of the City Hotel, where Pauline stayed upon her return.

Local newspapers covered the celebration on their front pages. Crowds of admirers filled the streets and soldiers on horses saluted the new heroine. The ladies from a local patriotic club presented

Pauline a handmade Union blue dress with epaulets attached showing the rank of Major.

The Union newspaper declared Pauline what the soldiers in the field were calling Pauline . . . Major Pauline Cushman. The rest of her life Pauline was addressed as "The Major."

Chapter Forty-Four

Nashville and the Future President

Pauline stayed in her room at the City Hotel in Nashville for the next two weeks. She then moved to the boarding house of Mrs. Pearl Swartz, a good Union lady, who traveled from St. Germain, Wisconsin to follow the 1st Wisconsin volunteer unit where her son served his country. Garfield regularly visited both the hotel and the boarding house. General Garfield kept Pauline on the U.S. Government payroll for the entire time.

Pauline was loved by the South after her toast and hated by the North. Now the North loved her and the South hated her. Consequently, even though she had powerful friends, and lovers, she had powerful enemies. She needed the protection afforded her by General Garfield's generous protection. Soon, Pauline had a new enemy from whom she needed protection: Lucretia Garfield.

Ladies had always been an important part of Garfield's life, but never a serious threat to his marriage. Like many wives of powerful men, Lucretia enjoyed her status and put up with his cheating behavior. This was different. Lucretia had her own spies who kept an eye on her husband while she was back in Ohio. Word came to Lucretia that Garfield fell head over heels for Pauline. Not the same old lustful James . . . a headstrong, giddy, laughing, joyful, James.

One evening when Garfield and Pauline were dining in Pauline's room a woman entered the sitting room at the front of the house.

"Who's there? Can I help you?" Garfield asked.

The lady didn't answer. She placed a beautiful cake on the table, turned and went out the front door. "Pauline, look at this cake. It looks delicious, would you like some?"

"Oh, James, I'm so satisfied...no thank you." Pauline wore a sheer yellow chiffon lounging dress and sat on the couch the two of them had been sharing.

"Well if we aren't going to enjoy the treat, I'll give a piece to Pearl's dog." Garfield reached down and gave the small beagle a nibble. The dog ate the nibble and begged for a larger portion.

"Here you are, old dog, don't beg me for more."

The dog didn't do any more begging. Ever again. The next morning, Garfield rose from his sleep and opened the guest house door to fetch the newspaper. The beagle lay stiff and lifeless on the porch floor.

"Pauline, don't touch that cake," he snapped as he stepped back into the house.

General Garfield and General Rosecrans scheduled a tour of middle Tennessee where Union forces were stationed after Bragg's retreat. They inspected the field hospital in West Nashville and reviewed local troops.

"Jim, my wife's arriving today. Why don't you invite Lucretia to join us for a joint review of the troops?"

"It's a good idea Will, I'll ask Lucretia to bring our daughter with her."

Garfield sent a telegram but Lucretia declined the invitation. The evening Garfield received Lucretia's refusal, he curled up on Pauline's couch encircling her shoulders.

"Look at you, you're left handed." he said.

"I know I'm left-handed," Pauline said. "So are you."

"You were poor when you were born, then rich, then poor. Me, I was just poor . . . raised in a log cabin," Garfield said.

Pauline stroked his left hand and kissed it.

"So, what else do we have in common?" Garfield said.

"Well, you speak German, Greek, and Latin. I speak Spanish, French, and Ojibwa."

"Ojibwa? The Ottawa Indian language? I don't think that counts." Garfield teased.

"Count? A whole nation speaks it . . . nobody speaks Latin, although you're old enough, maybe you did when you were young . . . "

Garfield laughed. He and Pauline were like kids together. He found her easy and non-judgmental. She found him protective and strong.

"What else?" Garfield asked.

"Well, people might laugh at us if we told them, but you and I both fear God," Pauline said.

"You've got that right, Pauline. I may not be a faithful husband, but I promised to take care of my wife for life. If I had my way, I'd spend every day of my life with you instead."

"Oh, don't be so dramatic, Jim. You're a great politician and you're going to do great things for this country. I'd get in your way. I know your plans can't include me. We've got tonight and maybe tomorrow. Stay here tonight, make love tomorrow, I'll hold your memory when you go away," Pauline responded.

Pauline added, "Besides, you may want to be a little more faithful and avoid your wife's baked goods."

***

The next morning, Garfield packed a small bag containing personal items he kept at Pauline's quarters. "Pauline, I'm going to leave you today and won't be back again," he said as he held her in his arms. She knew it would be their last . . . last kiss . . . last time they would ever hold hands . . . last time they'd ever make each other feel that way.

"This war is hell but it brought us together. I'll always be thankful for that," Pauline said.

She raised herself on tip-toes. She held her lips almost kissing him. After a moment, she placed hers on his and left them slowly caressing in tiny cupping motions.

She placed her body against his. Pauline lifted her head back and said, "You'll save our country and I'll be your fan. If I've done any brave thing in this war, it's here and now. I won't try to keep you, although I cried all night with the agony of your departure. You'll go and I'll find my way without you."

Garfield's tears fell from his eyes. "I love you. I'll let you go for your sake as well as mine. If I held you it would be as a mistress . . . not what you deserve. I might be able to talk you into that but at a price we'd both regret."

Garfield may not have been a faithful lover to Pauline, but he was a grateful and generous one. After speaking with Truesdail and General Granger, he expressed his feelings to General Rosecrans and President Lincoln. The following report is found in the War records, National archives:

Miss Cushman was employed by William Truesdail, Chief of the Army Police, to make a trip within enemy lines. After many acts of bravery on behalf of her country she was captured by rebel cavalry. She was tried, convicted and ordered to be hung. The enemy was routed from its stronghold leaving Miss Cushman sick and alone. General Granger found her and ordered her removed to Nashville.

Garfield subsequently wrote to President Lincoln: "This brave raven-eyed lady risked her life, and almost paid the ultimate price for loyalty to the Union has been dubbed, 'The Major' by local soldiers. I have made her a brevet Major and hope you approve of the measure."

President Lincoln, who was apprised of Pauline's bravery wrote, *"Let her keep this title as a reward for her service."*

Pauline then happily read some more good news from The Nashville Daily Press:

"PRISONERS- within the last day or two, the following men have been captured and turned over to the Provost Marshal: Benj, Milam, citizen, said to have been instrumental in the capture of Miss Cushman some time ago. He has also been trafficking with the Confederates."

The man who turned her in as a spy received his just reward.

Pauline thought about a favorite line from Shakespeare: "If you wrong us shall we not seek revenge?"

"Actions have consequences," she said aloud as she read the paper.

Now her name and face were known to both sides of the Mason-Dixon Line.

Pauline took her honors and her fame to the door of P.T. Barnum, the greatest showman of his time. While Pauline hoped to keep fighting for the Union in some way, the fighting continued without her. Pauline used a great number of men in her travels from Creole child, to famous actress, to celebrated spy.

She had affairs with Captain Blincoe, Colonel Moore, Colonel Truesdail, Sam Davis, young rebel spy, Titus, the Rebel jailer, Colonels Carter and Starnes, The list continued: Generals John Hunt Morgan, Nathan Bedford Forrest, and Braxton Bragg. And, at last, a man who would validate all of these episodes as legitimate actions for the good of her country, the Future President of the United States, General James A. Garfield.

Chapter Forty-Five

Where Did They Go?

On the fourth of July, 1863, two of Pauline's lovers, Colonel Moore and General John Hunt Morgan, met at Tebb's Bend in Kentucky. Moore and the men of Michigan's 25th came upon Morgan's troops. Morgan asked Moore to surrender. Moore said American's don't surrender on the fourth of July. They fought and Moore's group soundly defeated Morgan. At the end of Morgan's Raid from Kentucky to Indiana, they captured Morgan and imprisoned him.

Pauline told me she was distraught that he might die a prisoner. Pauline went to see him in that Yankee prison. She now was the free person while Morgan was the prisoner. She told me more than once she cared for Morgan and would have been that soldier's wife if he had asked.

It didn't matter what her feelings about slavery were, or his feelings about loyalty to his state. She blossomed in his company and longed for him long after they separated. She knew she did many things she'd never think of except for the sake of her country, but John Hunt Morgan was one soldier too many to ask of her. She told me she was entitled to one passionate love. So much pretending. So much seduction. So much heartache and loneliness. As she said, not alone, but lonely.

She entered the prison where Morgan was held under heavy guard one afternoon in late 1863. That evening, after the visit, Morgan used tools to break out and with some of his men, escaped from his cell.

She said the letter Bragg coerced from her and gave to Morgan was recognized for what it was. She never told me she provided the tools, but she cared for him so, I believe she did. It turned out their goodbyes in the prison would be their last. They recaptured Morgan shortly after his escape by a surprise encounter. He died with his men in battle.

Forrest fought until the end of the war. He started the Ku Klux Klan.

Bragg suffered through his many ailments and survived the war. His difficult nature continued. The Union government confiscated Bragg's property, leaving him penniless.

New Orleans appointed him superintendent of their waterworks, but he was replaced shortly thereafter. Bragg worked for Jefferson Davis as an agent for the Carolina Life Insurance Company. He lasted four months. The City of Mobile hired him to improve the river. He left after quarreling with a "combination of capitalists." He moved to Texas, and worked as the chief engineer of the Gulf, Colorado and Santa Fe Railway. He had a disagreement with the board of directors and resigned.

At the age of fifty-nine, Bragg walked down a street with a friend in Galveston, Texas. He fell over unconscious. He was dragged into a drugstore and died within minutes. Pauline didn't hold many grudges, but when this news reached her, she said, "His judgment day didn't come soon enough."

***

The war heightened all of her experiences. Regularly finding herself in circumstances where bullets, imprisonment, or death lurked changed her perspective. Quick decisions made all the difference. It seems the war that took lives of brothers, cousins, and neighbors took the hopes and dreams of victims in more ways than statistics show.

It was 1864. Pauline went from Creole kid, to Ottawa playmate, to runaway actress. From New York to New Orleans and back to Cleveland. Her husband lost, kids left behind, and a new spy career.

She had made love to the most powerful men in the country, lost men along the way who she cared for, and now, spun out of the army, she would re-invent herself.

Pauline was thirty-one years old. She was still a beautiful woman. If she couldn't make a living as a spy, she'd make a living as a teller of spy stories from her favorite place on earth . . . the stage.

Chapter Forty-Six

Off the Field and On the Stage

The Great Western Sanitary Fair, established to raise money for Union Troops, opened December 21, 1863. The Chairman of the event was General William Rosecrans. In The General's opening remarks he acknowledged Pauline's contribution to the Union cause.

"She braved the danger and went through my lines . . . gone longer than expected, we looked anxiously for her return; but she didn't come. At last when we took Shelbyville, we found her. She had escaped prison and she looked to find us. She was condemned to death as a spy! We rescued her in time and sent her to Nashville. I gave her all the money permitted me from public funds, a small amount indeed.

"This morning I received a card from her saying she wanted to see me. She wanted to know if I could pay her bill for boarding here, and pay her fare to return home. And now I'm going to give you the opportunity to show your appreciation for her devotion, by contributing something to relieve her present necessities."

People generously gave $300. The same money she received when she accepted the bribe from the Southern sympathizers to become a spy. General Rosecrans gave Pauline, still beautiful, some great attention. He arranged for her to speak at Mozart Hall. She earned some fees for her recitation and realized she could make a living after being a secret spy . . . by being a public one.

More than two thousand people paid twenty-five cents a ticket and added several hundred more dollars to her income. In 1863 a Major in the Union Army received seventy dollars per month.

Pauline tasted the thrill of big money that came with her celebrity.

General Rosecrans and General Garfield continued to be close friends. One or both of them watched over Pauline. Rosecrans, however, no longer commanded the army, having to take command of the Department of Missouri. Garfield was now in Washington, D.C. at the request of Abraham Lincoln. The President needed Garfield's support in the U.S. House of Representatives. Garfield resumed his elected position. Pauline needed to help herself start her new career as a show person. She would use her acting skills to perform and have a script written to make the performance interesting to her audiences.

Could Pauline travel the country on speaking tours and raise her children? She hadn't seen her kids since December of 1862. It was over a year and she missed them. She had money from the Sanitary Fair performances. Enough to get her to Vermont and more.

Her mother-in-law no longer could care for the children. Pauline's sister-in-law, Mary, cared for Ida. Pauline's other sister-in-law, Anne Newton, in Saxton's River, Vermont watched over little Charlie. Pauline told me she kept in contact with her two sisters-in-law who raised her children, but it wasn't pleasant. Pauline made trips to see Charlie and Ida but both sisters-in-law followed the Dickenson tradition. They didn't like Pauline. Her children, Pauline said, had been "poisoned against her."

Both children died in their youth, long before Pauline was able to care for them. Pauline never talked about her children in public but cried about them in private.

By the time Pauline's public life ended, her chance to be a mother to them ended as well.

This was late 1863. Her post-spy world had just began. She needed pamphlets written and printed, photographs taken, and props made for her presentations. Her first two performances were thrilling, but she knew she had to become professional if she wanted to continue to draw audiences.

Her theater experience taught her the shows had to be varied to keep audiences interested over a long time.

She tried Woods Theater in Louisville, as well as theaters in Nashville, and New York. Pauline reached out to the theater publicity agents. She found a friend who spent hours in Pauline's company and in return drew up and printed Pauline's pamphlets.

Photography studios were plentiful. It seemed every soldier, Union or Confederate, wanted to be memorialized by the camera. Brady's Photo Studio took several pictures of Pauline in her Major's Uniform and in formal attire in exchange for showing copies of her photos in their advertisements.

Adoring women from Nashville made her original Major's uniform. Later versions were produced by tailors from time to time as needed. It took her a month to put all of her presentation material together. Now she had to book engagements. This was way out of Pauline's experience and comfort zone.

Suddenly her luck changed for the better. Luck came in the person of an accomplished young Irish actor, James Ward. He was five years younger than Pauline, but she seemed to have a natural fitness that belied her age even with her occasional bouts with the bottle.

Chapter Forty-Seven

James Ward, New York City, and P.T. Barnum

New York theaters already respected James' talent. He drew audiences to theater doors when he traveled the country.

"Mr. Ward, you seem to be a darling of this crowd."

"Hi, Miss Cushman. I'm a great fan of yours. You really wowed the audience with your presentation."

This started a seven year relationship. James Ward had been more famous than Pauline up until the time of Pauline's toast to Jefferson Davis. Ward was an Irishman who took the New York stage by fire. Managers sought Ward for new plays and successful plays that needed new stars to keep their popularity. He may have been the better actor, but his immediate attraction to Pauline was no act. He fell for her during their first meeting.

Pauline had been through true loves, affairs and physical liaisons for her own advantage. She no longer was naive or easily flattered. She, however, felt a real draw to this dashing young man who brimmed with confidence and charming words.

"You were exciting on stage. Are you going to make more appearances?"

"I'm working on a production right now. I need to have pamphlets, photos and more before I'm ready. Frank Sarmiento has agreed to split the profits with me if he can write my biography."

Ward wasn't much taller than Pauline. He had strawberry blonde hair like Orlando Moore, but his hair was thick and curly, not like her balding ex-lover. The couple shared a drink in the cafe outside of the Grand Hall of the Sanitary Fair. Pauline had just pocketed even more money than her earlier performance proceeds.

"I'm booked to perform in Cincinnati for the next several days. Maybe when you have put your promotion together we could talk about booking performances as a team."

Pauline was surprised by the offer.

"I know you have no trouble working the theater in plays, but what will you gain by working with me?"

James warmed to the question and smiled his big Irish smile.

"I'm a comedian at heart. I have a comedy routine that will let me make a great solo living instead of worrying about the quality of the play, the other actors or whether the theater manager will stiff me." Pauline recognized this as a sincere offer, or at least a sincere semi-offer.

"So you want to be a fledgling solo performer just like me." Ward ordered two more drinks from the waiter.

"I'm famous for my acting. You're famous for your spying. I think our joint fame could draw enough people to our doors while we perfect our performances."

Pauline thought the idea had a lot of promise.

"Who would do our booking? Do you know anything about that side of the business?"

James paid the waiter, took a sip of his bourbon, neat, and paused.

"I have enough contacts with theater managers to get us started. We'll build a little success and then find a promoter who can get us some serious bookings."

Not so bad, Pauline thought. A few months ago I worried what a rope would do to my pretty neck. Now I'm sitting with a famous actor with money in my pocket and a plan for my new career.

Ward was true to his word. He contacted some managers who liked working with him. They promoted the joint act and the audience loved it. Ward turned out to be a funny guy on stage. He soon broadened his reputation and became the lead act in their two person show. Pauline had gone from Moore to Blincoe, to Truesdail to Gardner in a very short time. She never thought of herself as a tramp even when her motives for sleeping with a man were as necessary as a stagecoach ride or a riverboat ride. But she had enough. She wouldn't sleep with James Ward simply because he was attractive or because their joint show seemed mutually beneficial.

"Look Jim, we get along so well. I'm attracted to you, but I'd like not to complicate our working relationship. Can you handle that?" She surprised him. Women had always been attracted to him. An eighteen-year-old bonnie lass seduced him at age fourteen. He never needed to approach women thereafter, they always came to him.

"Sure. As long as you don't mind me being with other women from time to time, I won't mind if you don't want to be intimate with me. Let's shake on it."

Jim put his hand out to receive Pauline's. She rose from the table, took his hand, and kissed him on the cheek.

"That's a deal."

The deal lasted for a month. During that time the couple performed all over the Midwest, waiting for their chance to hit the big time stages. New York was their goal. Pauline had no more contacts in New York, but Jim did. He booked their act into the Keene Theater, the place Pauline started her professional career in 1852. The manager, Arnold Schmidt, died and John Broughman moved back to London.

After their performance in the summer of 1864 a man came to their dressing rooms . . . Phineas T. Barnum.

"Miss Cushman, I want to have you use your honorary title of Major Cushman at the American Museum for the next several months. How does that sound to you?"

Pauline had been with the greatest Generals of the United States, both North and South. She bedded the head espionage officer in the country as well as a future president of the United States. She wasn't easy to impress any more.

"Mr. Barnum, it's an honor to have you watch our performance. Of course we're flattered you'd want us, but we seem to be doing pretty well on our own."

Barnum liked her spunk. Pauline was thirty one. Barnum was sixty-eight. He was talking to a girl younger than his daughter.

"You may be doing pretty well, but have you heard of Jenny Lind? I made her an offer she couldn't refuse, even as big a worldwide star as her. She sang at the American Museum for many months at a fabulous salary. I'll pay the two of you what I paid her."

Pauline, not easily impressed, was impressed. Jim was stunned . . . both were happy.

They agreed to the arrangement and made an appointment to sign contracts in the next several days. That night amid champagne and caviar, the business partners slept in the same bed. They didn't change that arrangement for years thereafter.

Pauline, with P.T. Barnum's promotional genius, became internationally known. The home of Jenny Lind, the Fiji Mermaid, and Tom Thumb became the home of Major Pauline Cushman, Heroine of the Civil War. She and Ward became wealthy for the times. Their income surpassed most of the theatrical stars of the day. No one knows how they spent their money, but they started drinking more and missing performances.

After their engagement at the American Museum they traveled to Boston and Philadelphia.

Pauline had long been out of touch with General James Garfield who had given up his commission to return to Congress. To her surprise, she received a telegram at the theater where she and Jim performed in New York City. It said: *The President of the United States Desires your Company as soon as you can arrange to be at the White House, Washington, D.C.*

Chapter Forty-Eight

President Abraham Lincoln

Pauline finished her bookings in New York in 1864. She and Jim were headed to Philadelphia for a three week engagement. Pauline left the war when she traveled from Nashville to Cincinnati. Lincoln had no such privilege. Atlanta had fallen to Union troops in September and Nashville had elections that would put in another unionist government, but the war still continued. For every victory, there seemed to be another raid that would prolong the inevitable.

Lincoln managed the war from the White House but he also managed the politics of the war. Pauline was a symbol of Northern resilience. A star who didn't have to join the war effort took as dangerous a position as any officer in the service. She performed with honor, and was sentenced to hang. She handled that tragedy with resilience and tenacity. Her struggles were the struggles of the Union. Her victory from the gallows was a victory for the Union. To continue her fame made good political sense. With that thought in mind, the six foot four, craggy faced, stooped postured, President of the United States met with the beautiful statuesque Creole kid from New Orleans, turned national hero.

"Good morning Pauline Cushman. I have followed your career since Louisville."

"Good morning Mr. President. I have admired you since I lived in Cleveland. I can't believe I am in your presence, but, as God is my witness, this is the proudest day of my life."

This wasn't a presentation in front of Congress. The meeting took place in one of the office rooms of the White House. A secretary wrote down the conversation. The President carried a piece of paper in his hand.

"My life started in humble beginnings. Congressman Gardner has spoken of you with affection and respect. He advises me you've overcome great adversity in your life and have made your country proud."

The President paused. Pauline dabbed her eyelids with her handkerchief. Jim Ward stood in the back of the room, allowed to be present but silent.

"I'll read from this certificate, signed by my authority as President of the United States: *Pauline Cushman, for exemplary bravery in the face of the enemy, and with the thanks of a grateful Nation, I, Abraham Lincoln, hereby appoints you to the honorary rank of Major in the United States Army.*

Abraham Lincoln, President of the United States of America, October 14, 1864."

"Mr. President, I'll treasure this moment until my breath is taken from me. I pray you'll guide the Union to a land without slavery, and a land of peace. God bless you."

The President admired the young lady's composure. He paused to wipe a tear from his eye. He regained his composure, extended his hand to Pauline, gave a slight bow, and exited through the office door. Pauline went to Jim. He held her in an embrace of love, friendship, and admiration.

Pauline and Jim traveled the East Coast of the country until 1870 when Pauline turned thirty-seven. As people turned away from the war, Pauline became a reminder of many things audiences wanted to forget. Her recitations had no new stories to tell and bookings were no longer worthwhile.

Jim Ward's popularity as a comedian waned but his fame as an actor continued. Pauline had been the equal of generals. The equal of everyone she knew. She couldn't continue being a distant second to her actor boyfriend no matter how much she cared for him. Ward stayed in New York City and Pauline headed west.

Chapter Forty-Nine

Life after the Lime Light

Pauline told me she tried several cities hoping to find a new location and a meaningful life. She found herself in San Francisco in 1872.

She stopped writing to me, and the letters I sent were returned because of an incorrect address. She later said she was humiliated because she couldn't help herself, let alone help me.

Sometime in the years between 1870 and 1872 Pauline met Dr. Samuel Orr, a surgeon discharged from the Union army in 1863 due to a disability. By the time Dr. Orr's name appears in articles linked with Pauline, he was once again connected to the service as a civilian doctor on the government payroll.

After one of her performances at the Metropolitan, a reporter from the Alta California Newspaper interviewed her at a reception.

The interview in the next day's edition described Pauline beneath this Advertisement: *Sensational Actress Miss Major Pauline Cushman, known in the War of the Rebellion as the Scout of the Cumberland.*

The article said:

"She was prepossessing and attractive. In feature she shows plainly the marked characteristics of the French and Spanish blood which she inherits from her parents. Her lustrous and expressive black eyes, together with her animated and mobile countenance surrounded by soft raven hair, make up a most exciting image."

Pauline's future reviews of her acting in plays were not as full of praise as she would have wished. She played parts familiar to her from her acting days with James Ward, but to little applause.

Pauline's companion, Dr. Orr, stayed in adjoining rooms at the Grand Hotel during Pauline's performance. They had a romantic relationship. Rice, a teenage boy who worked at the hotel and became friends with Pauline and Dr. Orr, described their parting:

"Dr. Orr's exodus brought tears . . . When his stage rolled southward Miss Cushman retired to her rooms and refused to see anyone for several days. Even the theater had to wait and audiences held their tickets and fumed and fretted for several days."

Pauline continued to travel and lecture. Her audiences were smaller as her draw now seemed to be from the veterans of the Grand Old Army and the auxiliary organizations that kept memories of glory alive. Coupled with declining interest, Pauline suffered more bouts of illness causing her to cancel many performances.

She wrote to me once again in the year she married August Fitchner. He died and left Pauline a widow within a year. She next contacted me when she managed the La Honda hotel in San Mateo, California, south of San Francisco.

Dr. Orr moved out of her life, but Mickey Rice, the teenager who fell in love with Pauline, stayed on as her aide. Mickey told me in a letter:

"Bill Sears owned the hotel. He, like everyone else appreciated the Major's beauty, but unlike others, he tried to use his position as her employer. One night, following a performance, he met the Major in the hallway leading to her dressing room. He pushed her against the wall and kissed her. Pauline pushed him back and without saying a word entered her room. He leaned against the wall and swore beneath his breath. I halted opposite him and glared with all my might.

'You big stuff,' I said. He stared and gave me a dirty look.

'Don't bother with him, Mickey,' Pauline said calmly, 'he isn't worth it.'

"Pauline cancelled the rest of her performances and packed her things.

'You're being stupid,' Sears said.

"The Major turned her back on him and walked to the opposite end of the platform. I sat upon the luggage to face him. He glared at me and doubled his fists, but the presence of other people on the platform saved me from a beating.

"A short time later with a clatter of wheels and hoofs, the stage pulled up to a dust raising halt.

"Pauline went up to the driver and had a short conversation. The driver nodded, smiled, and handed her a long, blacksnake whip. She thanked him for the whip and holding the whip behind her, approached the man she loathed. The Major raised her skirt slightly with her left hand and with her right brought the whip down across his head and shoulders. He staggered and yelled with fright while the bystanders on the platform gazed with astonishment. A man tried to wrench it from her hand but her strength and speed were too much for him. She tired after several minutes, and left her victim a bleeding mass in the dust. The Major looked at him for a moment with expressionless eyes, then turned and handed the whip back to the dumb-founded driver.

'Thank you, sir,' she said. She nodded to me. 'Get in the stage Mickey, we're leaving.'

"I rose, picked up the baggage and obediently followed her into the vehicle's musty interior."

* * *

She wrote next in 1876. She wrote to me on her forty-third birthday. Pauline sent me money when she was performing for P.T. Barnum. Her generosity let me finish my degree at the University of Michigan. Now it was my turn. I sent her enough money to travel from San Francisco to Arizona and find a place to live.

She said she met the thirty-year-old handsome Jere Fryer, a fighter and scrapper like Pauline. They married in 1879.

A contributor to the Casa Grande newspaper tells about one of her Arizona adventures.

"Once a rattle-brained cuss became enraged at some imaginary wrong and took it into his fool head to blow up the town with nitroglycerine. He got five cases of the stuff in one of the stores, lit a fuse attached to a stick of TNT on top of the pile and then stood the town off with his gun.

The boys rather hated to kill him but the sputtering fuse had to be put out, so a delegation concluded to shoot him. Just then, Pauline Fryer came on the scene. She coolly ran up the pile of TNT, and regardless of the crazy fellow and his pistol, pulled out the fuse and threw it away. The startled man put down his gun and walked away."

Pauline wanted to have a child in her life. She befriended a lady who couldn't keep her child without a family scandal. She went away with the lady about the time her pregnancy would have shown. She returned with her baby, Emma. The baby delighted Pauline and Jere, but she died at the age of seven.

The child's death devastated Pauline and Jere Fryer. They were living separately before Emma's death but their chances of reconciliation vanished when Emma passed away.

In the last years with Jim Ward, the two of them drank too much. Pauline never beat the addiction. She tried to be a mother again and failed. She had no more children, and apparently no new friends. She passed away in 1893. Articles in all of the major newspapers recalled her heroics when they published her obituary.

People remember her contribution to the victorious Union cause and her defense of peace in the Arizona Territory. I remember her as my big sister who watched over me all of her life.

Chapter Fifty

Conclusion

People may judge my sister by her actress vagabond lifestyle. Certainly Pauline had failings. She might have handled her marriage and motherhood in a different fashion. She might have found her way without using men for her purposes.

But Pauline, the little near-white girl from New Orleans met and dealt with the biggest personalities of her times as an equal. Her bravery in the face of death is undisputed. The information she provided the Union forces undoubtedly saved hundreds if not thousands of Union soldiers. The country made her a star of the stage as an actress, a star in the war as a spy.

She told me many tales about her sense of right and wrong, and her willingness to risk her life in pursuit of right. Her own physical frailty, however, started to rule her life.

At her best, her countrymen owed her praise. Because she was a woman, her feats were looked on as a woman's accomplishment, not on a larger scale had a man accomplished the same feats. As big a place as Pauline had in her own times, her legacy might have been the equal of Rosecrans and Bragg, Forrest and Morgan, had she been a man.

So it was the way of Pauline Cushman. In a smaller way than Lincoln or Grant certainly, but in a significant way, with genuine integrity. She had genuine intentions to make a difference in her world. Her lifelong strength and determination made the lives she affected better for having known her.

In her youth, she loved Abram, the Ottawa Indian and her beloved Charlie. She became a spy; fell for General Morgan and thereafter

General Garfield. She lived several more years, toured the United States telling of her exploits, and had many people write about her adventures. Pauline's popularity faded as people turned away from the war. She left Mr. Barnum, headed west and eventually remarried ... twice.

Fame does strange things to most of us. Pauline had a pure heart and an honest desire to help her country. She loved the stage. She loved the notoriety of being a "Major" in the army. As other attractions took center stage, Pauline drank. She married a fellow who drank.

Garfield and President Lincoln saw that Pauline had a small pension for her service to the Union. Lincoln might have done more for her had he lived. Garfield caused her to receive the title of Major and promoted her pension claim to Lincoln.

Shortly after Pauline's affair, Lucretia Garfield contacted her friends in the Ohio Republican party to talk to her husband.

The Republican Party loyalists finally convinced him to put aside his adulterous ways if he wanted to run for higher office. After his life and Pauline's life were put in danger, he recognized his wife meant business. By the time Garfield became president in 1881 Pauline was almost fifty years old, and just a memory to him.

Pauline went from back woods tomboy to an American celebrity. She had an influence in the lives of Rosecrans, Bragg, John Hunt Morgan, Nathan Bedford Forrest, James A. Gardner, and Abraham Lincoln. She continued, through hard work and determination, to stay in the national spotlight from 1863 until 1870. She continued as a local celebrity almost to the end of her life.

Pauline's life forms part of the history of our Civil War. She was a poster child for significance as a woman in a man's world. She understood the evil of prejudice because she felt it as a young girl. Her bravery, genuine fervor for life and her accomplishments during our county's greatest conflict make her story worth the telling by me, and the reading by everyone who appreciates that freedom comes at a cost to those needing to be free.

Chapter Fifty-One

Short Biographical Sketches of Notable Persons Appearing in Pauline's Biography

"**P.T. Barnum*** was an American showman and businessman remembered for promoting celebrated hoaxes and for founding the Barnum & Bailey Circus. Although Barnum was also an author, publisher, philanthropist, and for some time a politician, he said of himself, "I am a showman by profession . . . and all the gilding shall make nothing else of me," and his personal aim was "to put money in his own coffers." Barnum is widely, but erroneously, credited with coining the phrase "There's a sucker born every minute."

He embarked on an entertainment career, first with a variety troupe called "Barnum's Grand Scientific and Musical Theater," and soon after by purchasing Scudder's American Museum, which he renamed after himself. Barnum used the museum as a platform to promote hoaxes and human curiosities such as the Fiji mermaid and General Tom Thumb. In 1850 he promoted the American tour of singer Jenny Lind, paying her an unprecedented $1,000 a night for 150 nights. After economic reversals due to bad investments in the 1850s, and years of litigation and public humiliation, he used a lecture tour, mostly as a temperance speaker, to emerge from debt. His museum added America's first aquarium and expanded the wax figure department.

During the Civil War, Barnum's museum drew large audiences seeking diversion from the conflict. He added pro-Unionist exhibits, lectures, and dramas, and he demonstrated commitment to the cause. In 1864 Barnum hired Pauline Cushman to lecture about her "thrilling adventures" behind Confederate lines. Barnum's Unionist sympathies incited a Confederate arsonist to start a fire in 1864."

http://en.wikipedia.org/wiki/P._T._Barnum

"**Lieutenant Colonel Edward Bloodgood*** held Brentwood, a station on the Nashville & Decatur Railroad, with 400 men on the morning of March 25, 1863, when Confederate Brig. General Nathan B. Forrest, with a powerful column, approached the town. The day before, Forrest had ordered Col. J.W. Starnes, commanding the 2nd Brigade, to go to Brentwood, cut the telegraph, tear up railroad track, attack the stockade, and cut off any retreat.

Bloodgood sought to notify his superiors and discovered that the telegraph lines were cut. Forrest sent in a demand for surrender under a flag of truce but Bloodgood refused. Within a half-hour Forrest killed 350 of Bloodgood's 400 soldiers."

* *http://americancivilwar.com/statepic/tn/tn015.html*

"**General Jeremiah Boyle*** was a successful lawyer and noted abolitionist. He served as a brigadier general in the Union Army. At the outbreak of the Civil War, Boyle raised a brigade of infantry for service in the Union Army. He was commissioned as a brigadier general on November 19, 1861. After wintering his troops in Tennessee, he joined Maj. Gen. Don Carlos Buell's Army of the Ohio and participated in the Battle of Shiloh.

He resigned in 1864 after his son, the Union Army's youngest colonel, Col.

William O. Boyle, was killed in action at the Battle of Marion in Tennesee. He had been affectionately known as 'the Boy Major.'"

*http://en.wikipedia.org/wiki/Jeremiah_Boyle

"**General Braxton Bragg*** was a career United States Army officer, and then a general in the Confederate States Army—a principal commander in the Western Theater of the American Civil War and later the military advisor to the Confederate President Jefferson Davis.

Bragg, a native of North Carolina, was educated at West Point and became an artillery officer. He served in Florida and then received three brevet promotions for distinguished service in the Mexican-American War, most notably the Battle of Buena Vista. He established a reputation as a strict disciplinarian, but also as a junior officer willing to publicly argue with and criticize his superior officers, including those at the highest levels of the Army.

In 1863, he fought a series of battles against Maj. Gen. William S. Rosecrans and the Union Army of the Cumberland. In June, he was outmaneuvered in the Tullahoma Campaign and retreated into Chattanooga. This retreat allowed Pauline Cushman to escape her pending execution. In September, he was forced to evacuate Chattanooga, but counterattacked Rosecrans and defeated him at the Battle of Chickamauga, the bloodiest battle in the Western Theater, and the only major Confederate victory therein. In November, Bragg's army was routed in turn by Maj. Gen. Ulysses S. Grant in the Battles for Chattanooga.

Throughout these campaigns, Bragg fought almost as bitterly against some of his uncooperative subordinates as he did against the enemy, and they made multiple attempts to have him replaced as army commander. The defeat at Chattanooga was the last straw and Bragg was recalled in early 1864 to Richmond, where he became the military adviser to Confederate President Jefferson Davis."

*http://en.wikipedia.org/wiki/Braxton_Bragg

"**John Broughman*** He managed the Lyceum theatre, for which he wrote several light burlesques. He moved to the United States, where he acted and became a member of W.E. Burton's company, for which he wrote several comedies. He opened Brougham's Lyceum from which he wielded much local power in the New York theater world."

*http://en.wikipedia.org/wiki/John_Brougham

"**Charlotte Cushman*** was an American stage actress. Her voice was noted for its full contralto register, and she was able to play both male and female parts. During the last six years of her life Cushman developed a remarkable ability as a dramatic reader, giving scenes from Shakespeare, ballad poetry, dialect poems and humorous pieces with a success not less decided than her earlier dramatic triumphs."

*http://en.wikipedia.org/wiki/Charlotte_Cushman

"**Lieutenant General Nathan Bedford Forrest*** was a general in the Confederate Army during the American Civil War. He is remembered as a self-educated, brutal, and innovative cavalry leader during the war and as

a leading Southern advocate in the postwar years. He was a pledged delegate from Tennessee to the New York Democratic national convention of 4 July 1868. He served as the first Grand Wizard (head of movement) of the Ku Klux Klan, but later distanced himself from the organization.

A cavalry and military commander in the war, Forrest is one of the war's most unusual figures. Although less educated than many of his fellow officers, before the war Forrest had already amassed a fortune as a planter, real estate investor, and slave trader."

*http://en.wikipedia.org/wiki/Nathan_Bedford_Forrest

"**General James A. Garfield*** After Abraham Lincoln's election as president, several Southern states announced their secession from the Union to form a new government, the Confederate States of America. Garfield read military texts while anxiously awaiting the war effort, which he regarded as a holy crusade against the sin of Slavery. In April 1861, the rebels bombarded Fort Sumter, one of the last federal outposts in the South, beginning the Civil War. Although he had no military training, Garfield knew his place was in the Union Army.

Following a trip to Illinois to purchase muskets, Garfield returned to Ohio and, in August 1861, received a commission as a colonel in the 42nd Ohio Infantry regiment.

He was the 20th President of the United States, serving from March 4, 1881, until his assassination later that year. Garfield had served nine terms in the House of Representatives, and had been elected to the Senate before his candidacy for the White House, though he declined the office once he was president-elect.

He recommended Pauline Cushman to receive the honorary title of "Major." Lincoln accepted his recommendation and made the proclamation in the White House with Major Pauline Cushman at attention.

Garfield's accomplishments as president included a resurgence of presidential authority against senatorial courtesy in executive appointments, energizing American naval power, and purging corruption in the Post Office, all during his extremely short time in office."

*http://en.wikipedia.org/wiki/James_A._Garfield

"**General Joseph Johnston*** was a career U.S. Army officer, serving with distinction in the Mexican-American War and Seminole Wars, and was also one of the most senior general officers in the Confederate States Army during the American Civil War. He served in Florida, Texas, and Kansas, and fought with distinction in the Mexican-American War and by 1860 achieved the rank of brigadier general as Quartermaster General of the U.S. Army. When his native state of Virginia seceded from the Union, Johnston resigned his commission, the highest-ranking officer to join the Confederacy. To his dismay, however, he was appointed only the fourth ranking full general in the Confederate Army."

*http://en.wikipedia.org/wiki/Joseph_E._Johnston

"**Laura Keene** was a British stage actress and theatre manager. In her twenty-year career, she became known as the first powerful female manager in New York. She is most famous for being the lead actress in the play *Our American Cousin*, which was attended by President Abraham Lincoln at Ford's Theater in Washington, D.C., on the evening of his assassination."

*http://en.wikipedia.org/wiki/Laura_Keene

"**Abraham Lincoln*** despite being little prepared for it by prior military experience, was first and foremost a war president. The nation was at peace for less than six weeks of his presidency and it was the only presidency that was entirely "bounded by the parameters of war". Lincoln was called on to handle both the political and military aspects of the war, and his leadership has to be evaluated based on his ability to balance these inseparable parts of the Union's efforts. He was a successful war president to the extent he was able to control the revolutionary forces unleashed by his election and Southern secession, maintain the democratic principles that were the bedrock of the nation, and achieve a military victory. His assassination five days after the end of the war left the final challenge of reconstructing the nation to others, but Lincoln as early as 1863 established principles he felt should shape this process. Lincoln, as commander-in- chief, suspended habeas corpus for prisoners suspected of supporting the Southern cause."

* http://en.wikipedia.org/wiki/Presidency_of_Abraham_Lincoln

"**Brigadier General John Hunt Morgan*** was a Confederate general and cavalry officer in the American Civil War. Morgan is best known for Morgan's Raid when, in 1863, he and his men rode over 1,000 miles covering a region from Tennessee, up through Kentucky, into Indiana and on to Southern Ohio. This would be the farthest north any uniformed Confederate troops penetrated during the war. The success of Morgan's raid was one of the key reasons the Confederate Heartland Offensive of Braxton Bragg and

Edmund Kirby Smith was launched later that fall, assuming tens of thousands of Kentuckians would enlist in the Confederate Army if they invaded the state.

Morgan was promoted to brigadier general on December 11, 1862, He received the thanks of the Confederate Congress on May 1, 1863, for his raids on the supply lines of Union Major General William S. Rosecrans. He made the longest raid into Union territory of any Confederate soldier. Morgan and his exhausted, hungry and saddle sore soldiers were finally forced to surrender.

November 27, Morgan and six of his officers, escaped from their cells in the Ohio Penitentiary. The raid was in direct violation of his orders from General Braxton Bragg."

*http://en.wikipedia.org/wiki/John_Hunt_Morgan

"**Colonel Orlando Hurley Moore*** was in several battles but he is most famous for his defeat of John Hunt Morgan in The Battle of Tebbs' Bend. The battle was fought on July 4, 1863, some days after the escape of Pauline Cushman from General Bragg's headquarters. Despite being badly outnumbered, elements of the Union Army thwarted repeated attacks by Morgan's dismounted cavalry."

*http://en.wikipedia.org/wiki/Battle_of_Tebbs_Bend

"**William Starke Rosecrans*** was an American inventor, coal-oil company executive, diplomat, politician, and U.S. Army officer. He gained fame for his role as a Union general during the American Civil War. He was the victor at prominent Western Theater battles, but his military career was effectively ended following his disastrous defeat at the Battle of Chickamauga in 1863.

Rosecrans was a graduate of West Point who served as a professor at the academy and in engineering assignments before leaving the Army to pursue a career in civil engineering.

Given command of the Army of the Cumberland, he fought against Confederate Gen. Braxton Bragg at Stones River, and later outmaneuvered him in the brilliant Tullahoma Campaign, driving the Confederates from Middle Tennessee. Shelbyville was abandoned by Bragg, leaving Pauline to find her way back to Union territory."

* http://en.wikipedia.org/wiki/William_Rosecrans

"**Colonel James Starnes*** was a prominent physician and planter. He graduated from a medical school in Louisville, Kentucky. He served as a surgeon in the Mexican War. When the Civil War started, he raised a company of cavalry in Tennessee. Starnes was promoted to colonel and led a brigade of Forrest's Cavalry. He was successful in his raid on Brentwood, together with General Forrest. During the Tullahoma Campaign that freed Pauline Cushman, he was mortally wounded by a sharpshooter."

http://www.findagrave.com/cgi-bin/fg.cgi?page=gr&Grid=17790418

"**Colonel William Truesdail** was a successful railroad executive and businessman. He was brought to service by General William Rosecrans. Allan Pinkerton, the famous detective, had Truesdail's job until Lincoln fired General George B. McClellan. Pinkerton quit his post in protest. Truesdail accepted the position.

From his Nashville, Tennessee headquarters he commanded two hundred spies and scouts within his department. He personally trained Pauline Cushman to be a spy. When the Union forces were going to overrun Shelbyville, Bragg's headquarters and the site of Pauline's confinement, Truesdail sent ninety of his scouts to rescue her."

Afterword

The Author used Wikipedia and other on-line sites from Gov.org to many Civil War websites and blogs. A project of this nature required extensive research. I am grateful for the twenty-first century tools that allow an author to spend less time in libraries, and more time writing. Notwithstanding, many historical items have not yet reached the internet, so old-fashioned rummaging through dusty volumes still consumed this author's time.

Bibliography

Ash, Stephen V. Middle Tennessee Society Transformed 1860-79, *War and Peace* in *the Upper South*. Baton Rouge: Louisiana State University Press, 1988.

Ambrose, Stephen E. *Nothing Like it in the World*. New York: Simon and Schuster, 2000.

Barnum, Phineas T. *Life of P.T. Barnum*. New York: Redfield, 1854. Barnum, Phineas T. *Struggle and Triumph, or, Forty Year' Recollections*. Buffalo: Warren, Johnson and Company, 1873.

Baxter, Albert J. *History of the City of Grand Rapids*. New York and Grand Rapids: Munsell and Company, 1891.

Blanton, DeAnne, and Lauren Cook. *They Fought Like Demons*. Baton Rouge: Louisiana State University Press, 2002.

Blum, Daniel J. *A Picture History of the American Theater, 1860-1970*. New York: Crown Publishers, 1971.

Boatner, Mark. *The Civil War Dictionary*. New York: David McKay and Company, 1959.

Bradley, Michael. Tullahoma: *The 1863 Campaign for the Control of Middle Tennessee*. Shippensburg: Burd Street Press, 2000.

Brandes, Ray. Frontier Military Posts of Arizona. Globe, Arizona: Dale Stuart King, 1960.

Brown, Dee Alexander. Morgan's Raiders, New York: Konecky and Konecky, 1959.

Burnham, Frederick R. *Scouting on Two Continents*. Garden City, New York: Doubleday, Doran and Company, 1928.

Campbell, Reverend John P. *Nashville Business Directory*. Nashville: Smith Camp and Company, 1857.

Chambers, Robert W. *Secret Service Operator, 13*. New York: Appleton-Century Company, 1934.

Cleveland City Directory. Cleveland: Spear, Denison and Company, 1855-1856

Coleman, Penny. *Spies! Women in the Civil War.* Cincinnati: Betterway Books, 1992.

Connolly, James A. *Three Years in the Army of the Cumberland*, Bloomington: Indiana University Press, 1959.

Cozzens, Peter. *This Terrible Sound: The Battle of Chickamauga.* Urbana and Chicago: University of Illinois Press, 1959.

Dannett, Sylvia. *She rode with Generals: The True and Incredible Story of Sarah Emma Seeley.* New York: Thomas Nelson and Sons, 1960.

Dorman, James H. Theater in the Antebellum South, 1851-1860. Chapel Hill: University of North Carolina Press, 1967.

Dudden, Faye E. *Women in the American Theatre.* New Haven: Yale University Press, 1994.

Durham, Walter T. *Reluctant Partners: Nashville and the Union.* Nashville: Tennessee Historical Society, 1987.

Durham, Walter T. *Nashville, the Occupied City.* Nashville: Tennessee Historical Society, 1985.

Dyer, Frederick H. *A Compendium of the War of Rebellion*, Des Moines, Iowa: Dyer Publishing Co., 1908.

Edmonds, S. Emma E. *Nurse and Spy in the Union Army.* Hartford: W S. Williams and Company, 1865.

Elliot, Sam Davis. *Soldier of Tennessee.* Baton Rouge: Louisiana State University Press, 1999.

Faust, Patricia, editor. *Historical Times Illustrated Encyclopedia of the Civil War.* New York: Harper and Row, 1986.

Leonard, Elizabeth A. The Daring of the Soldier. New York: W. W. Norton and Company, 1999.

Loomis and Talbot's Cleveland City Directory. Cleveland: Herald Office Printer, 1861.

Mabie, Hamilton Wright, and Kate Stephens, eds. *Heroines That Every Child Should Know*: Tales for Young People of the World's Heroines of All Ages. E.C.S.K. Series. New York: Doubleday, Page, 1907

Manitowoc County Historical Society. *The Flag of Company A, Fifth Wisconsin Volunteer Infantry, 1861-1925.* Manitowoc, Wisconsin: Manitowoc County Historical Society, 1928.

Markle, Donald E. *Spies and Spymasters of the Civil War.* New York: Hippocrene Books, 1994.

Mary Elizabeth. *Bonnet Brigade,* New York: A. A. Knopf, 1966.

Massey, Mary Elizabeth. *Women in the Civil War.* Lincoln, Nebraska: University of Nebraska Press, 1996.

Mayorga, Margaret G. *A Short History of the American Drama.* New York: Dodd & Mead, 1944.

McClintock, James H. *Arizona, Prehistoric, Aboriginal, Pioneer, Modern: The Nation's Youngest Commonwealth Within a Land of Ancient Culture,* Vol. 3, 175-76 Chicago: The S. J. Clarke Publishing Co., 1916.

McKenney's Business Directory *The Principal Towns Central and Southern California, Arizona, New Mexico and Southern Colorado.* San Francisco: Pacific Press Publishing, 1883.

McWhiney, Grady. *Braxton Bragg and the Confederate Defeat, Volume 1, Field Command.* New York: Columbia University Press, 1969.

Metz, Leon C. *El Paso Chronicles.* El Paso, Texas: Mangan Books, 1993.

Miers, Earl Schenck, ed. Lincoln Day by Day, a Chronology, 1809-1.865, Volume IIL 1861-1865. Washington, D.C.: Lincoln Sesquicentennial Commission, 1960.

Michigan Federal Census Index, 1850. Lansing: Genealogical Commission, Michigan State Library, 1976.

Miller, Francis Trevelyan. *The Photographic History of the Civil War, Vol. 8.* New York: Thomas Yoseloff, reprint 1957.

Moore and DePue's *Illustrated History of San Mateo County, California, 1878.* Oakland, California: Moore and DePue, 1878.

Moore, Dennis R., editor. *The Papers of James S. Anderson.* Madison: State Historical Society of Wisconsin, 1989.

Moore, Frank. *Women of the War: Their Heroism and Self-Sacrifice.* Hartford: S. S. Scranton, 1867.

Muscatine, Doris. *Old San Francisco.* New York: G. P. Putnam's Sons, 1975. Myrick, David F. *Railroads of Arizona,* Vol. 1. Berkeley: Howell-North Books, Oxford University Press, 2002.

Odell, George C. D. *Annals of the New York Stage.* New York: Columbia University Press, 1931.

O'Neil, James. *History of San Francisco Theatre*. San Francisco: California State Department of Education, 1942.

Payne, William. *Cleveland Illustrated, a Pictorial Hand-book of The Forest City*. Cleveland: Fairbanks, Hendrick and Company, 1876.

Peskin, Allan. *Garfield*. Kent, Ohio: Kent State University Press, 1999.

Poland, O. A. *Poland's Columbus Directory and Classified Business Mirror for 1864*. Columbus: O. A. Poland, 1864.

Quebbeman, Frances E. *Medicine in Territorial Arizona*. Phoenix: Arizona Historical Foundation, 1966.

Radley, Kenneth. Rebel Watchdog: *The Confederate States Army Provost General*. Baton Rouge: Louisiana State University Press, 1989.

The Racine City Directory. Racine: Smith, Du Moulin and Company, 1858. Ray, Grace Ernestine. Wiley Women of the West. San Antonio: The Naylor Company, 1972.

Reflection: *A Pictorial History of Fremont, Nebraska 1870-1920*. Fremont, Nebraska: Friends of the Fremont Opera House, 1977.

Regnery, Dorothy F. *The History of Jasper Ridge, From Searsville Pioneers to Stanford Scientists*. Palo Alto: Stanford Historical Society, 1991.

Reinders, Robert C. *End of an Era, New Orleans, 1850-60*. New Orleans: Pelican Publishing Company, 1964.

Revett, Marion S. *A Minstrel Town*, New York: Pageant Press, 1955

Robbins, Millie. *Tales of Love and Hate in Old San Francisco*. San Francisco: Chronicle Books, 1971.

Robertson, John, compiler. *Michigan in the War*. Lansing: State of Michigan Adjutant General's Office, W. S. George and Company, 1882.

William Ganson. *Cleveland, the Making of a City*. Cleveland: World Publishing Company, 1950.

Sarmiento, Ferdinand L. Life of Pauline Cushman. Philadelphia: The Keystone Publishing Company, 1865

Swearengin, John A. Good Men, Bad Men Lawmen, and a Few Rowdy Ladies. Florence, Arizona: John A. Swearengin, 1991.

Sweeney, Edwin R., editor. Making Peace with Cochise, the 1872 Journal of Captain Joseph Alton Sweeney. Norman: University of Oklahoma Press, 1997.

Sword, W. Wiley. *Shiloh: Bloody April*. New York: William Morrow and Company, 1974.

Tennessee State Directory, Volume 2, 1873-74. Nashville: Wheeler, Marshall and Bruce, 1873.

Thrapp, Dan L. *Encyclopedia of Frontier Biography*, Vol. I. Glendale, California: Arthur H. Clark Company, 1988.

Tierney, Tom, *Famous African-American Women Paper Dolls.* New York: Dover Publications, 1994.

U.S. War Department. *War of the Rebellion: The Official Record of the Union and Confederate Armies.* Washington, D.C.: War Department, 1889-1901.

Weist, John J. *Theatre of Louisville, Kentucky Known Variously as Mozart Hall, Wood's Theatre and the Academy of Music.* Louisville: John Jacob Weiset, 1962.

Wiley, Bell Irvin. *Life of Billy Yank: The Common Soldier of the Union.* Baton Rouge: Louisiana State University Press, 1952.

Wilson, Garff, B. *A History of American Acting.* Bloomington, Indiana: Indiana University Press, 1966.

Wilson, Garff, B. *Three Hundred Years of American Drama and Theatre.* Englewood Cliffs, New Jersey: Prentice-Hall, 1974.

Wilson, James and John Fiske, editors. *Appleton's' Cyclopedia of American Biography.* New York: D. Appleton and Company, 1888

Woodworth, Steven E. Jefferson Davis and His Generals: The Failure of Confederate Command in the West. Lawrence, Kansas: University of Kansas Press, 1990.

Wyatt, Roscoe D. Historical Place Names in San Mateo County. San Mateo, California: San Mateo County Historical Association, 1947.

Wyeth, John A. *Life of General Nathan Bedford Forrest.* Dayton: Morningside Bookshop, reprint 1975.

Wyeth, John A. *That Devil Forest; Life of General Nathan Bedford Forrest.* Baton Rouge: Louisiana State University Press, reprint 1989.

Yater, George H. *Two Hundred Years at the Falls of the Ohio: A History of Louisville and Jefferson County.* Louisville: The Filson Club, 1987.

Young, John V. *Ghost Towns of the Santa Cruz Mountains.* Santa Cruz: Western Tanager Press, 1984.

Young, Agatha. *The Women and The Crisis: Women of the North in the Civil War.* New York: McDowell, Oblensky, 1959.

Made in the USA
Charleston, SC
13 October 2016